AWAKENING
TO THE VIOLENCE OF
SYSTEMIC RACISM

AWAKENING TO THE VIOLENCE OF SYSTEMIC RACISM

Vince Gallagher
and Sherine Green

Paulist Press
New York / Mahwah, NJ

Cover photo by Stephen Voss
Cover design by Sharyn Banks
Book design by Lynn Else

Library of Congress Cataloging-in-Publication Data
Names: Gallagher, Vincent A., author. | Green, Sherine, author.
Title: Awakening to the violence of systemic racism / Vince Gallagher and Sherine Green.
Description: New York ; Mahwah, NJ : Paulist Press, [2021] | Includes index. | Summary: "*Awakening* bears witness to the most egregious disparities between African American people and white people caused by the structural injustice inherent in virtually every institution in the United States. The authors help white people see and understand how the deck has been stacked against people of color. Their eye-opening research leads to deeper understanding of what Black people have suffered and to seeing without excuse the very real harm caused by racism"—Provided by publisher.
Identifiers: LCCN 2021007939 (print) | LCCN 2021007940 (ebook) | ISBN 9780809155668 (paperback) | ISBN 9781587689659 (ebook)
Subjects: LCSH: African Americans—Social conditions. | Race discrimination—United States. | United States—Race relations. | Racism—United States. | Racism—Religious aspects—Catholic Church. | Social justice—Religious aspects—Catholic Church.
Classification: LCC E185.61 .G35 2021 (print) | LCC E185.61 (ebook) | DDC 305.896/073—dc23
LC record available at https://lccn.loc.gov/2021007939
LC ebook record available at https://lccn.loc.gov/2021007940

ISBN 978-0-8091-5566-8 (paperback)
ISBN 978-1-58768-965-9 (e-book)

Published by Paulist Press
997 Macarthur Boulevard
Mahwah, New Jersey 07430
www.paulistpress.com

Printed and bound in the
United States of America

What the eye doesn't see, the heart doesn't feel.

—Haitian proverb

CONTENTS

FIGURES

FOREWORD

Awakening Is the First Step toward Racial Justice and Healing

Rasheda L. Weaver, PhD

The time is right for *Awakening*.

America is experiencing an explosion of consciousness related to racism in our country. I call it an explosion of consciousness because many of us thought we were in a post-racial society.

In 2008, the United States made history when President Barack Obama became the nation's first African American president. People throughout the world rejoiced and had a new sense of hope. Their celebration and hope stems from their painful knowledge of the experience of African Americans—some of the most oppressed, brutalized, and terrorized people in world history. Thus, witnessing an African American man and his beautiful and loving family rise to the most powerful office in the world became the highlight of many people's lives, including my own. Many of us feel that if he could accomplish the impossible then maybe we can too.

While the Obama era illustrated that African Americans could reach the highest of heights, the Donald J. Trump era that followed .awakened the world to the fact that America's racist history was not just that—history. The racist, sexist, xenophobic behaviors of Trump's presidential campaigning followed him into the White House and throughout his entire presidency, erupting into a period of heightened racial tension and violence in the country.

From the beginning until the very end, millions of Americans and people across the globe protested the administration and its incitement of racial violence. It has been a volatile time for America. However, it taught Americans something very important: Racism is very much real and it has no boundaries. It influences every aspect of African American life.

Awakening to the Violence of Systemic Racism does an excellent job of illustrating the multidimensionality of racism in the United States. It describes how anti-Black racism affects housing, healthcare, childbirth outcomes, food access, employment opportunities, educational outcomes, and more. As such, the knowledge brought forth in *Awakening* is not only needed but also essential to advancing racial healing.

As a scholar of community development and entrepreneurship, I must tell you that the first step toward solving any problem is to acknowledge its existence. Once we recognize a problem exists, we can then work to solve it.

Awakening to the long-standing, systemic, and complex problem of anti-Black racism in the United States is of paramount importance to setting the foundation needed to combat it. America needs to acknowledge, examine, and develop *effective* interventions against racial injustice and violence. Once again, racism has no boundaries. As discussed throughout this book, racism affects every aspect of African American lives, and thus interventions are needed in every aspect of American life.

I laud Vince Gallagher and Sherine Green's refreshing yet raw exploration of systemic racial violence in *Awakening*. Their work advances reader racial and cultural competence, while also giving readers permission to explore their own experiences with racism regardless of their color or race.

Vince's honest account of witnessing systemic and local racism while living and working in Camden, New Jersey, and Philadelphia, Pennsylvania, tell a story of how racism can be subtly taught and accepted, but that people can still intentionally unlearn racism. Sherine's many experiences, as a Black and Indian Jamaican woman who has lived in several white-dominated countries, highlight the fact that anti-Black racism and racial inequities exist throughout the world. As such, while this book focuses on the African American experience, its lessons are relevant to people everywhere.

A topic in the book that is of particular importance to racial healing is solidarity. The authors discuss how solidarity is achieved when people who have different experiences and viewpoints come together to sort them out in an effort to build community. My hope for Americans is that we, as a people, build solidarity by becoming more preventive as opposed to reactionary when it comes to racism. We shouldn't just protest when we feel African Americans or others have been unjustly murdered. We must create a culture and a group dynamic where hatred, stigmatization, bias, injustice, and violence against African Americans are not tolerated and are harshly punished.

In addition, we, as a people, must come together to foster human well-being overall, not just regarding the issues that affect us directly. The truth is that all issues faced in our country are related.

As Dr. Martin Luther King Jr. said, "We are caught in an inescapable network of mutuality, tied in a single garment of destiny. Whatever affects one directly, affects all indirectly." History has taught us that people who are hell-bent on oppressing others rarely have limitations. They start with one group, then move on to the next.

My hope is that after all we have been through as a nation, people start to internalize Dr. King's message and truly come together in solidarity. Though we have had some rough, eye-opening years, I am proud of the progress we have made as a nation. As explored in *Awakening*, once upon a time in the United States, Black people were enslaved and lynched, and it was normal and even celebrated. Today, slavery is abolished, and when Black people get murdered it is protested and, for the most part, punished with imprisonment.

While our society is far from where it needs to be, no amount of progress made should ever be taken for granted. America recently made history again when it elected President Joe Biden and Vice President Kamala Harris, the first Black person and first female to serve as vice president. This administration has made a commitment to fighting racial injustice, and that should give us all hope. The fact that Americans voted for them in record numbers during the middle of the coronavirus pandemic should give us all hope. And I urge anyone committed to fighting racism to take no amount of progress for granted. Every win is a win.

We are now in a new era focused on addressing racial injustice and advancing our nation's healing. Thus, *Awakening* comes at the right time. By recognizing the tragedies of our past, while highlighting the progress of our present, *Awakening* has the potential to enlighten us into a better future.

Thank you, Vince Gallagher and Sherine Green, for bringing this gift to our world.

PREFACE

We wrote *Awakening* because of our experience of teaching hundreds of groups of middle-class and upper-class white students and parish groups at the Romero Center in Camden, New Jersey. We learned that most participants have only a superficial understanding of the notion of systemic racism. We also found that among the young people, there is growing hunger for justice not seen before the Black Lives Matter movement. We believe that hunger has come from young hearts being broken open by the suffering of George Floyd, Breonna Taylor, Rayshard Brooks, Freddy Gray, Eric Garner, Tamir Rice, and so many others.

Working to repair and restore justice in virtually every institution and organization is of paramount importance. There will be no lasting, meaningful systemic change, however, until the hearts of all white people, especially those in positions of power, have been opened to all of their sisters and brothers.

Hearts are opened by understanding. We hope that *Awakening* contributes to your growth in understanding, compassion, and love so your hunger for justice deepens. We pray that as your hunger deepens, you will find the best ways to use your gifts to serve and become an instrument of healing and love.

ACKNOWLEDGMENTS

We would like to thank Michele Szachewicz for all of her administrative help in putting together the manuscript and book. It simply would not have happened without her. We are grateful for the encouragement, inspiration, and advice of Kathleen Furin. Her guidance was essential in creating *Awakening*.

We are also indebted to the many researchers and authors on whom we relied. Their work involved many long hours of digging up and exposing the facts that show the magnitude, severity, and insidiousness of the harm of racism embedded in virtually every institution and organization in the United States. Those to whom we are most appreciative include Michelle Alexander, author of *The New Jim Crow: Mass Incarceration in an Age of Colorblindness*. She, more than anyone we know, opened the door for the world to see how politicians, legislators, and judges have created a caste system to continue to control and punish African American people through the criminal justice system. Likewise, Alexandra Natapoff, author of *Punishment without Crime*, shows clearly and specifically how the criminal justice system and so many other institutions have targeted African American people for punishment of misdemeanors, tremendously disproportionate to white people.

Richard Rothstein, author of *The Color of Law: The Forgotten History of How Our Government Segregated America*, has performed meticulous research that has revealed the history of the ways our government has created a caste system to control and separate African American people from white people. Carol Anderson, author of *One Person, No Vote: How Voter Suppression Is Destroying Our Democracy*, shows specifically how, since the end of slavery to the present, politicians and legislators have been preventing

African American people from voting. Edward E. Baptist, author of *The Half Has Never Been Told: Slavery and the Making of American Capitalism*, shows that the suffering and death of so many African American people served as massive fuel for the growth of the industrial revolution and the creation of wealth enjoyed by white people today.

We are also most grateful for the extensive research provided by the Equal Justice Initiative, the Civil Rights Project at UCLA, the Brennan Center for Justice at New York University School of Law, the Economic Policy Institute, the Institute for Policy Studies, the American Civil Liberties Union, the Southern Poverty Law Center, the United Church of Christ Commission for Racial Justice, Human Rights Watch, and others.

Many authors have written books that have been key in opening our hearts and minds to the ways so many precious people have been harmed in so many ways by systemic racist policy. We are grateful for their inspiration. A few of the most important are

- James Baldwin, *The Fire Next Time, Nobody Knows My Name, If Beale Street Could Talk*
- Ta-Nehisi Coates, *Between the World and Me*
- James H. Cone, *Black Theology and Black Power, Black Theology of Liberation*, and *Said I Wasn't Gonna Tell Nobody*
- Ben Crump, *Open Season: Legalized Genocide of Colored People*
- Eddie S. Glaude Jr., *Democracy in Black: How Race Still Enslaves the American Soul*
- Paul Kivel, *Uprooting Racism: How White People Can Work for Racial Justice*
- Bryan N. Massingale, *Racial Justice in the Catholic Church*
- Melvin L. Oliver and Thomas M. Shapiro, *Black Wealth/White Wealth: A New Perspective on Racial Inequality*
- Tavis Smiley, *The Covenant with Black America— Ten Years Later*

Acknowledgments

- Jemar Tisby, *The Color of Compromise: The Truth about the American Church's Complicity in Racism*
- James Wallis, *America's Original Sin*
- Harriet A. Washington, *Medical Apartheid: The Dark History of Medical Experimentation on Black Americans from Colonial Times to Present*
- Augustus A. White III, MD, *Seeing Patients: Unconscious Bias in Healthcare*

We are both deeply indebted to all the African American people whose lives and stories are embedded in the statistics, that is, the unspeakable suffering caused by racism: separations of families, insults, beatings, rapes, tortures, mutilations, lynchings, incarcerations, and so many needless deaths that have led to our hearts being opened more and more.

INTRODUCTION

Few members of the oppressor race can understand the
deep groans and passionate yearnings of the oppressed
race.

> —Reverend Martin Luther King Jr.,
> Letter from Birmingham Jail,
> April 16, 1963

We have been called, chosen, and sent to live here on this broken
planet and to awaken to the kingdom of God that is "before us"
and "within us" so that we grow in love of God and others and
care for one another. A terrible truth is that one powerful way
that our love is awakened is when our hearts are broken open by
the suffering of others—when we realize how precious people
are harmed and treated unfairly.

Hasidic Rabbi Levy Yitzhak of Ukraine tells this story. The
rabbi visited the owner of a tavern. Two peasants were at the
table. They were drinking with reckless abandon with arms
around each other saying how much they loved each other.
Ivan said to Peter, "Peter, tell me what hurts me?" Weary-eyed
Peter looked at Ivan, "How can I know what hurts you?" Ivan's
answer was swift, "If you don't know what hurts me, how can
you say you love me?"

If understanding is not there, no matter how hard you try, you
cannot love. If you say, "I have to try to love him," this is non-
sense. You have to understand him and by doing so, you will
love him....Without understanding, love is impossible.

> —Thich Nhat Hanh

1

You have probably noticed that living on this third planet from our sun is no easy matter. Even if you are born into a stable middle- or upper-middle-class family, it isn't so easy. Children can be tough on each other. Teenagers can be worse. Adults can be brutal. But it is a lot harder to get along when the people of the dominant culture think they are better than you and worse when they have stacked the deck against you.

Awakening is meant to help white people to see and understand how the deck has been stacked against people of color by opening their minds to a deeper understanding of the structural injustice and institutionalized violence of racism and by opening their hearts through a deeper understanding of the *harm* caused by racism.

An awakening of white people of all ethnicities and ages to the brutality of racism is beginning in response to the deaths of Ahmaud Arbery, Breonna Taylor, George Floyd, and so many others, and to the many weeks of protests by people supporting Black Lives Matter during the coronavirus pandemic. Only time will tell if lasting, meaningful transformation occurs.

The Emancipation Proclamation and the end of the Civil War led to the Ku Klux Klan, Jim Crow laws, Black Codes, convict labor, torture, massacres, lynchings, voter suppression, and on and on. The gains of the civil rights movement of the 1950s and 1960s led to a resurgence in hate crimes, killing of leaders of the National Association for the Advancement of Colored People (NAACP), bombings, and the killing of Black children. It led to the creation of a "new caste system" and the imprisonment of young African American men who, in some states, were arrested at rates twenty to fifty times greater than white men for the same drug offense. So the jury is out about the extent of the transformation that will occur in our laws and structures and in the hearts of white people.

Of *paramount* importance is the changing of the laws and policies of virtually every institution and organization. But if there is no corresponding change in the behavior and attitude of white people, especially those in power—Congress, CEOs, executives, university presidents, judges, government administrators, and others—there will be no meaningful, lasting change.

Introduction

There will be another backlash and more subtle yet effective ways to control people of color for economic gain.

A change in attitude and behavior follows a change of heart. A change of heart comes about as we get to know each other and "see" each other as real. A change of heart becomes possible when white people are able to "see" how racism has harmed and is harming *precious* people.

White people who live, worship, and work in largely segregated communities are likely to have little understanding of African American people and their culture, as well as the magnitude, severity, and insidiousness of the harm caused by racism. They are at risk of spiritual unconsciousness as a result of their blindness. They are at risk of perpetuating the structural injustice and the institutionalized violence of racism in which they participate and from which they have benefitted.

White people who have never experienced the insults of bigotry, prejudice, and discrimination will likely have only a *superficial* understanding of the way housing, educational, healthcare, legal, and economic structures and government policies, from which white people have benefitted for hundreds of years, are continuing to cause emotional, physical, and economic harm to African American people. They are likely to have little understanding of how the same historical forces that were created by our government to separate and control African American people during slavery and Jim Crow are still working today. They are at risk of suffering moral injury from their lack of understanding, compassion, and love.

Awakening tries to make clear *some* of the most egregious disparities between African American people and white people that have resulted because of the structural injustice inherent in virtually every institution in the United States. These structures, laws, and policies cause harm often unseen and unnoticed by white people.

People who fail to examine the root causes of the disparities between white and African American people may be comfortable thinking that the cause of poverty and the failure of many African American people to achieve success as they know it is because of their values rather than the values of the mostly

3

powerful white men who have created unfair structures and policies that disproportionately benefit white people. For instance:

- Being unaware of the historical disparities and injustices in funding of schools, in discipline, corporal punishment, the school-to-prison pipeline, toxic school environments causing learning disabilities from lead exposure, and so on, they may think that African American people are just not as intelligent as white people.
- Being unaware of the backlash of the civil rights movement and the magnitude of the mass incarceration of African American people, they may think that African American people commit more crimes than white people.
- Being unaware of the disparities in access to healthcare and treatment, they may think that African American people don't take as good care of their health as white people do.
- Being unaware of government affirmative action economic policies that disproportionately help middle- and upper-middle-class white people, they may think that most African American people earn less and have less wealth because they are not as ambitious as or just don't work as hard as white people.

Racism is not the result of what some bigoted white people say or do from time to time. The behaviors of bigotry are symptoms of racism. Racism results from white people's values, that is, the desire to control, dominate, exploit, and feel superior to African American people. Those values have created unjust structures designed to enhance power, control, and economic advantage.

Racism results from the values and actions of people in the legislative, executive, and judicial branches of our government. Those values have created a society that has controlled, taken advantage of, and harmed African American people for four hundred years. They have created residential segregation, segregation in education, mass incarceration of African American people, disparities in access to healthcare and in healthcare outcomes, voter suppression, disparities in income and wealth, and many other forms of control and injustice.

Our intent is to help you *see* and understand specifically how this system has been designed and implemented, and has subsequently caused so much harm for so long to so many people in so many ways.

> And now here is my secret, a very simple secret:
>
> It is only with the heart that one sees rightly; what is essential is invisible to the eye
>
> —Antoine de Saint Exupery

There are no people more important nor precious than others—certainly not in God's eyes. We have all come from God. We are infused with God's Holy Spirit. God's kingdom lies within each of us. We are truly temples of God's Holy Spirit and loved beyond measure. But when we look at each other, we often see differences that lead to judgments. We just don't yet have eyes to really "see" each other. One day at noon, Thomas Merton, a Trappist monk, was given the grace to really see as he looked at people at an intersection in Louisville, Kentucky:

> In Louisville, at the corner of Fourth and Walnut, in the center of the shopping district, I was suddenly overwhelmed with the realization that I loved all of those people, that they were mine and I was theirs, that we could not be alien to one another even though we were total strangers. It was like waking from a dream of separateness and spurious self-isolation in a special world….I almost laughed out loud….If only everyone could realize this!…There is no way of telling people they are all walking around shining like the sun.[1]

The goal of *Awakening* is simple: to be of help so that you can *see* more clearly and *love* more dearly. Chapters 1 and 2 are about the backlash that occurred as a result of the end of slavery and the passage of the Civil Rights Act of 1964. Significant gains were met with more subtle yet severe responses. In chapters 3 through 8, we have focused on only a very *few* of the most egregious ways our government and other institutions have created and administered racist laws and policies. We focused on the most severe tactics, especially those likely to be unknown to white people. Chapter 9 is about restorative justice—reparations and the role of the government. Chapters 10 and 11 are about the ways hearts can be opened by the power of story and prayer. At times, we have commented on injustice that impacts other people of color. However, racism toward Latin American people and other people of color is only touched on here as it is a topic for other books.

This book is meant to be only an overview of some of the most harmful examples of institutionalized violence suffered by African American people. It is meant to serve as a modest beginning for understanding. It in no way intends to be a comprehensive treatment of the ways African American people have been harmed through racism. A few of the topics related to injustices suffered by African American people that we do not cover are:

- the history of burning Black churches, which has been occurring for more than 150 years and continues today
- the growth of the KKK and the terror inflicted on African American people, including the recent growth of other hate groups
- the harm caused by medical experiments performed on African American people
- discrimination in labor unions, corporations, universities, banks, churches
- university admission policy
- how judges' decisions, including the Supreme Court, have caused harm to African American people
- disproportionate occupational injury, disease, and death suffered by people of color
- discriminatory treatment of African American women

- disproportionate capital punishment suffered by African American people
- media bias
- the long history of police brutality

Just read the newspapers and listen to the news. You will see the list goes on and on.

We have not provided guidance about ways to work for racial justice because that is the subject of many other books. We have provided a list of recommended books related to understanding and combating racism (see the appendix). At the end of each chapter, we have provided an excerpt of Catholic social teaching with questions for reflection and discussion, as well as questions to consider regarding responses to this injustice. Finally, there is an invitation to prayer at the end of each chapter.

> Don't let the lion tell the giraffe's story.
>
> —Nigerian proverb

We recognize that no white person can understand what it is like for an African American person to live in a racist society. But an old lion (Vince) can tell young lions about some of the ways lions—mostly white men—have designed the means to capture, control, punish, and make use of African American people. Sherine Green was the catalyst and inspiration for this book. She collaborated with Vince in planning and providing ideas, suggestions, and theological insight. As a Jamaican woman who has lived in white-dominated societies, Sherine knows well the story of the giraffe and the dangers of living in the "jungle." She has been a peacemaker and in many ways has served as a bridge between white people and people of color. She has witnessed the transformations that can occur when white people move out of their comfort zone and into the camp of the other. She tells some of her story in chapter 10.

Sherine and Vince met when Sherine worked at the Romero Center in Camden, New Jersey. Camden is one of the most impoverished cities in the United States. Middle- and upper-class students, mostly white, come to the Romero Center to spend a weekend or a week witnessing, serving, and learning the structural roots of poverty and considering the injustice they encountered in light of Catholic social teaching. Vince made presentations to the participants about his book *The True Cost of Low Prices: The Violence of Globalization*. It explains how the powerful, mostly white men, have organized global economic and political structures that are obscenely unfair to poor people and beneficial to mostly white people. The students learned something of structural injustice and institutionalized violence from which they benefit.

Sherine's life has been dedicated to fighting racism and working for justice. She has created many opportunities for white people to spend time together and get to know people of color. It is in the encounter and sharing of stories when hearts are broken open in compassion for our oppressed sisters and brothers that God's Holy Spirit and Jesus's love enters and inspires us to care, love, and serve.

Sherine and Vince became keenly aware that many of the white students they taught lived in isolation from people of color and had little understanding of their own blindness and how they and their families have benefitted from the injustice of racism. So this book was written for them and others who have a desire to learn about, awaken to, and respond to this injustice.

We trust that through prayer and the power of the Holy Spirit, you will be guided toward the best ways to use your particular gifts to respond. We hope that each of you will have your hearts opened more and more so that you naturally desire to respond more and more. It is really simple: We are called to grow in love and care for one another by sharing the gifts we have been given.

> Martin Luther King, Jr., called for us to be lovestruck with each other, not colorblind toward each other. To be lovestruck is to care, to have deep compassion, to be concerned for each and every individual, including the poor and vulnerable.
>
> —Cornel West

APPLICATION

Catholic Social Teaching

"Open Wide Our Hearts: The Enduring Call of Love," a pastoral letter against racism, from the United States Conference of Catholic Bishops, says,

> Too many good and faithful Catholics remain unaware of the connection between institutionalized racism and the continued erosion of the sanctity of life. We are not finished with the work. The evil of racism festers in part because, as a nation, there has been very limited formal acknowledgement of the harm done to so many, no movement of atonement, no national process of reconciliation, and all too often, a neglect of our history. Many of our institutions still harbor, and too many of our laws still sanction, practices that deny justice and equal access to certain groups of people. God demands more from us. We cannot, therefore, look upon the progress against racism in the recent decades and conclude that our current situation meets the standards of justice. In fact, God demands what is right and just.

Reflection & Discussion

How Well Do You Know African American People?

1. Is your church community integrated?
2. Do you or anyone in your extended family live in an integrated neighborhood?
3. Have your schools been integrated?
4. How many close African American friends do you have?
5. Have you ever been to a birthday party of an African American person?
6. How many African American people have visited your home?

7. Have you ever been to a funeral of an African American person?
8. Have you ever held an African American baby in your arms?
9. Are you among the millions of middle- and upper-middle-class white people who live to a large extent isolated from African American people and their culture?
10. Do you have a desire to know the stories of African American people?
11. Do you have a desire to open your heart and mind and to grow in love?

Prayer Invitation

Wake me up Lord, so that the evil of racism
finds no home within me.
Keep watch over my heart
and remove from me any barriers to your grace
that may oppress and offend my brothers and sisters.
Fill my voice, Lord, with the strength to cry freedom.
Free my Spirit, Lord, so that I may give services of
justice and peace.
Clear my mind, Lord, and use it for your glory
and finally, remind us, Lord, that you said
blessed are the peacemakers
for they shall be called children of God.
Amen.[2]

1

THE BACKLASH TO THE END OF SLAVERY

They put him to death by hanging him on a tree.

—Acts 10:39

CONTROL THROUGH JIM CROW LAWS

Racism can be defined as "racial prejudice plus power." It is based on the belief of the superiority of white people. Power and the belief of the superiority of white people have always been used against African American people to separate, control, and exploit. Enslavement was the most effective way of control, but not the only way.

After slavery, African American people had great hope that, with freedom, they would be paid for their work, be able to establish their own schools and churches, elect their own politicians, and establish their own communities. They did indeed begin to establish biracial governments in the South. Six hundred African Americans were elected to state governments, fourteen to the U.S. Congress, two to the U.S. Senate, and many others to lower offices, including judges and sheriffs. Reconstruction was enforced by federal troops that protected African American people and their newly obtained freedom and rights.[1]

In 1865, the Thirteenth Amendment abolished slavery except for punishment for a crime. In 1868, the Fourteenth

11

Amendment provided equal protection under the law. In 1870, the Fifteenth Amendment provided prohibition of racially discriminatory voter laws. African American people now had hope of using the right to vote to gain political power, access to jobs and better schools, and rights to own their land. This hope was a great threat to Southern whites. So a backlash began to grow. The first major mass murder occurred in the spring of 1866 in Memphis, Tennessee.

Memphis Massacre

After a shooting incident between white policemen and freedmen who fought in the Civil War, white officers began firing into a crowd of innocent African American men, women, and children who had gathered on South Street. Then white mobs rampaged throughout Black neighborhoods with the intent to "kill every Negro and drive the last one from the city." Over three days of violence, forty-six African Americans were killed (two whites were killed by friendly fire); ninety-one houses, four churches, and twelve schools were burned to the ground; at least five women were raped; and many Black people fled the city permanently.[2] The next major mass murder incident occurred less than three months later in New Orleans.

New Orleans Massacre

In New Orleans, a group of African Americans attempted to convene a state constitutional convention to extend voting rights to Black men and repeal racial discriminatory laws known as "Black Codes." Black Codes were vagrancy laws that allowed local authorities to arrest freed people for minor infractions and commit them to involuntary labor. The unemployed and homeless were considered vagrants. Even people considered to be loitering were arrested. Their most common fate was to be sold into forced labor.[3]

When the delegates to the constitutional convention convened at the Mechanics Institute on July 30, 1866, a group of Black supporters and white opponents clashed in the streets. The white mob began firing on Black marchers, indiscriminately killing convention supporters and Black bystanders. Rather than maintain order, white police officers attacked Black residents with guns, axes, and clubs, arresting many and killing dozens. By the time federal troops arrived to suppress the white insurgency, as many as forty-eight Black people were dead and two hundred had been wounded.[4]

Despite this violence, Black people became voters and wielded significant political power, especially in states and counties where they constituted majorities. This led to white people in power disputing election results, which often resulted in bloody massacres. In 1873, after a very close gubernatorial election, a militia of white Democrats killed dozens of Black Republicans in what came to be known as the Colfax Massacre.[5]

Colfax, Louisiana

In 1872, after several years of white Democrats fraudulently undermining the votes of Black Republicans, Black protestors refused to recognize their illegitimate election results. They staged a peaceful occupation of the town courthouse.[6] In response, in the first week in April 1873, approximately 140 whites surrounded the courthouse and fired shots. The outnumbered Black forces waved white flags in surrender, but the assault continued. The unarmed Black men who hid in the courthouse or attempted to flee were shot and killed. Approximately fifty Black men who survived the afternoon assault were taken prisoner and executed. As many as 150 African Americans were killed in the massacre, described as "the bloodiest single act of carnage in all of Reconstruction." No whites were held accountable because the U.S. Supreme Court dismissed all federal charges against them.[7] As you will see, this decision and many more like it by lower courts and the Supreme Court have resulted in the distrust that many African American people have today of our criminal justice system.

Ku Klux Klan

The earliest seeds of violent white resistance to Reconstruction were planted in Pulaski, Tennessee, in late 1865, when six Confederate veterans formed the Ku Klux Klan.[8] It quickly spread and developed a complex hierarchy with rules as intricate as an army manual. In less than a year, chapters spread throughout Tennessee and into Northern Alabama. Klan members came from every echelon of white society in the nineteenth century, including lawyers, merchants, and ministers. By the 1868 presidential election, those cells were poised to act as a unifying military force supporting the cause of white supremacy throughout the South.[9]

African American people were also controlled by various white groups that took up the cause of restoring "labor discipline" in the absence of slavery. Vigilantes whipped and lynched Black freed people who argued with employers, left the plantation where they were contracted to work, or displayed any economic success of their own.[10] White terror groups also controlled African American men by targeting them for perceived sexual transgressions against white women. Charges of rape, while common, were "routinely fabricated" and often extrapolated from minor violations of the social code, such as "paying a compliment" to a white woman, expressing romantic interest in a white woman, or cohabiting interracially.[11] White mobs regularly attacked Black men accused of sexual crimes. Historians estimate that at least four hundred African Americans were lynched between 1868 and 1871.[12]

SUPREME COURT'S SUPPORT OF RACISM

The Supreme Court participated in supporting racism by making racial discrimination legal. In the civil rights cases of 1883, the Supreme Court ruled that the Civil Rights Act of 1875, which prohibited racial discrimination in hotels, trains, and other public places, was *unconstitutional*. The court ruled that since slavery had been over for almost twenty years, Black people now needed to finally stand on their own without the help of the government, in spite of crippling poverty, daily violence, and the ascension of Jim Crow.[13] Justice Joseph B. Bradley wrote the majority opinion:

The Backlash to the End of Slavery

When a man has emerged from slavery, and, by the aid of beneficent legislation, has shaken off the inseparable concomitants of that state, there must be some stage in the progress of his elevation where he takes the rank of a mere citizen and ceases to be a special favorite of the laws, and when his rights as a citizen or a man are to be protected in the ordinary mode by which other men's rights are protected.[14]

The Supreme Court found that, despite the fact that Black people were subjected to continual racial discrimination, they did not warrant "unique consideration." Black people were now like everybody else, so they reasoned, and no longer needed the protection of the Civil Rights Act. Princeton Professor Eddie S. Glaude Jr. reports, "Tragically, more than two thousand people were lynched in the United States between 1882 and 1903. Didn't matter: the problem [racial discrimination] had been solved."[15]

Homer Plessy vs. Ferguson

Homer Plessy, a thirty-nine-year-old white shoemaker with a trace of African American blood, was arrested for riding in a white compartment on an East Louisiana railroad train. He was tried and convicted on a ruling that created the concept of "separate but equal" public facilities for Blacks and whites. Douglas Blackmon, in *Slavery by Another Name*, writes that the ruling certified that it was moral and legitimate to treat African American people unequally. It endorsed the doublespeak of Jim Crow segregation. It provided a justification for the new slavery that began with the passage of Black Codes resulting in convict labor.[16]

BLACK CODES AND CONVICT LEASING—SLAVERY BY ANOTHER NAME

The Thirteenth Amendment prohibits slavery "except as a punishment for a crime." So, Black Codes were passed to control freed people and to continue slavery. Black Codes are laws that make it very easy to convict African American people for crimes such as vagrancy, changing employers without permission, walking down the street without proof of employment, riding freight cars without a ticket, and loud talk with white women. The codes made it a crime for freed people not to sign contracts with white landowners and to sell cotton after sunset. It made it very easy to reestablish slavery.

Black Codes led to mass arrests and incarceration of African American people. The most common fate of the African American "convict" was to be sold into forced labor to profit the state. The convicted "freed" person was sold by the government to work in mines, labor camps, quarries, farms, steel mills, or factories. Hundreds of forced labor camps throughout the South were operated by state and county governments, large and small corporations, and farmers. Every former Confederate state except Virginia "leased" African American prisoners to work in conditions very similar to slavery.

As convict labor, African American people were treated brutally, unable to escape, almost always tortured, starved, and often literally worked to death in just a few years. If they did stay alive, they were subjected to never-ending rounds of indebtedness to whoever leased them. State governments made tremendous amounts of money from the system, in the coal mines, steel mills, timber operations, and vast cotton plantations; literally the entire economy of the South was dependent on convict labor.[17] The equivalent of tens of millions of dollars went into the state treasuries. Hundreds of thousands of African American men were captured and used in this neoslavery.

One example of the treatment of convict workers is indicated in a grand jury report in Hinds County, Mississippi, in 1887. It reported that six months after 204 convicts were leased to work for a man named McDonald, twenty were dead, nineteen had escaped, and twenty-three had been returned to the penitentiary disabled, ill, and near death. The Equal Justice Initiative (EJI) reports that countless African American men, women, and children lost their freedom—and often their lives.[18]

16

CONTROL THROUGH LYNCHING

Lynchings, often publicly, were routinely used from 1868 to 1950 to terrorize and kill African American people. EJI has documented incidents of mobs torturing and hanging African American people during 4,084 racial terror lynching incidents in twelve southern states and more than 300 incidents in other states between the end of Reconstruction in 1877 and 1950.

Alabama	361
Arkansas	492
Florida	311
Georgia	589
Kentucky	168
Louisiana	549
Mississipi	654
North Carolina	123
South Carolina	185
Tennessee	233
Texas	335
Virginia	84
TOTAL	4,084

Figure 1: African American Lynching Victims by Southern State, 1877–1950[19]

The lynchings were carried out with impunity, sometimes in broad daylight and often on the "courthouse lawn." Some public spectacle lynchings were attended by the entire white community. They were meant to publicize the extent to which white people would go to control African American people by terror, torture, and murder.

Tulsa Race Massacre

On May 31, 1921, Dick Rollin was in jail accused of raping an elevator operator in broad daylight in her elevator. Headlines in the local newspapers stirred up both white and Black people. A crowd gathered outside the courthouse, and a struggle between a white and a Black person resulted in a shot being fired. The massacre began.

Estimates are that between one hundred and three hundred African American people were murdered. But this we know for sure:

- In the Greenwood District of Tulsa, there were many prosperous African American businesses and families.
- Airplanes dropped firebombs on homes of African American families, destroying 1,256 homes.
- Virtually every other structure in the forty-square block area of Greenwood was destroyed: a dozen churches, five hotels, thirty-one restaurants, schools, businesses, a hospital, and the library.
- Public officials provided firearms and ammunition to white people.
- The Oklahoma National Guard participated in the mass arrests of nearly all of the Greenwood residents.
- There was no resistance to the massacre at any level of government.
- Not one of these criminal acts was ever prosecuted at any level: municipal, county, state, or federal.[20]

All it took to ignite this tremendous explosion of violence and evil within the white people of Tulsa was the "accusation" that a young Black man attempted to rape a white woman in a public elevator in broad daylight.

Today, most African American people know their history well. Many white people have little understanding of the extent of the brutality that white people used to subjugate and murder African American people. This ignorance helps maintain the notion of white supremacy. There will be little hope of white people recognizing how the structures of racial injustice that exist today are working without an understanding of how they have existed and how they continue to evolve to respond to changes. Without an understanding of this history, it can be difficult to see the sometimes more subtle methods of control and discrimination that are at play today. It is then also more difficult to recognize that incidents of members of the police killing innocent African American people today is a continuation of injustices that began four hundred years ago.

> Back in them days, to kill a negro wasn't nothing. It was just like killing a chicken or killing a snake. The whites would say, "Niggers jest supposed to die, ain't no damn good anyway—so jest go an' kill 'em."
>
> —James Cone, *The Cross and the Lynching Tree*

EJI found that most terror lynchings had one or more of the following features:

- resulted from the widely distorted fear of interracial sex
- were a response to casual social transgressions
- were based on allegations of serious violent crime
- were public spectacles
- escalated into large-scale violence targeting entire African American communities
- aimed to control sharecroppers, ministers, and community leaders who resisted mistreatment

Martin Luther King's first encounter with lynching occurred in a conversation with his parents. His father told him this story:

"What the hell are you laughin' at, nigger?" one man shouted. "I ain' laughin', suh, honest I ain't....Jus' on ma way home is all,..." He was in the wrong place at the wrong time. There was no exit. He was a scapegoat just like Jesus. "Nigger struttin' down the road like he thinks he's up North someplace. Pocket full of money. Laughin' at white folks." It was payday and they tried to take his money. "This money fo' my chil'ren now," the Black man screamed, fighting back. "I cain' let you have that." They proceeded to kick and beat him severely—"blood pouring out of the man's mouth," as he cried out in painful agony. "They pulled him right past me," Daddy King remembered; "it was as if I hadn't even been there watching." Then "one of them took off his belt and wrapped it around the Negro's neck. They lifted him up and tied the end of the belt to this tree and let him go...his feet about five or six inches off the ground." Like Jesus, hanging on a cross, this nameless Black victim, hanging on a Georgia tree, was left to die a shameful death—like so many other innocent Blacks, completely forgotten in a nation that did not value his life.[21]

Imagine how the child Martin's mind and heart would have been affected upon hearing this story of his ancestors told to him by his father. This story and hundreds of other stories of which he was well aware would ignite in his heart the Holy Spirit of Jesus, which guided his life. That same Holy Spirit can be ignited in everyone's heart.

Lation Scott

Another heinous incident involved the murder of Lation Scott in 1917 in Dyersburg, Tennessee. Scott was accused of "criminal assault." Thousands gathered near a vacant lot across the street from the downtown courthouse, and children sat atop their parents' shoulders to get a better view as Mr. Scott's clothes and skin were ripped off with knives. A mob tortured Mr. Scott with a hot poker iron, gouging out his eyes, shoving the hot poker down his throat, and pressing it all over his body before castrating him and burning him alive over a slow fire. His torturous killing lasted more than three hours.[22]

> Blessed are you who are persecuted for righteousness' sake, for theirs is the kingdom of Heaven.
>
> —Matthew 5:10

Thousands of people, mostly Christian, endorsed and supported this horrific murder and apparently saw no conflict with gospel values. Even today many white people fail to understand how insidious these systems of racial injustice are, how alive these terrifying memories are for the descendants of enslaved people who suffered these injustices. Many people worship on Sunday morning thinking the abuses of African American people are mostly in the past now that African American people have been given opportunities and, in some cases, perhaps even advantages that white people don't have. Some white people even believe there is more racism against whites than Blacks.[23] The Kaiser Family Foundation found that 57 percent of white people don't think racism is a big problem today.[24] This is evidence of people suffering from spiritual blindness. It is evidence of spiritual injury.

The gruesome public spectacle lynchings described above traumatized the African American community. The crowds of thousands of white people attending as participants or spectators included elected officials and prominent citizens. White press coverage regularly defended the lynchings as justified. Investigations rarely led to identification of lynch mob members, much less prosecutions. White men, women, and children fought over bloodied ropes, clothing, and body parts and proudly displayed these "souvenirs" with no fear of punishment.[25] In Newnan, Georgia, in 1889, pieces of Sam Hose's heart, liver, and bones were sold after he was lynched; that same year, spectators at the lynching of Richard Coleman in Maysville, Kentucky, took flesh, teeth, fingers, and toes from his corpse.[26] Spectacle lynchings were preserved in photographs that were made into postcards and distributed unashamedly through the mail.[27]

> God transformed lynched Black bodies into the resurrected Body of Christ. Every time a white mob lynched a Black man, they lynched Jesus. The lynching tree is the cross in America. When American Christians realize that they can meet Jesus only in the crucified bodies in our midst, they will encounter the real scandal of the cross.
>
> —James Cone, *The Cross and the Lynching Tree*

The following are just some of the many massacres of African American people:[28]

- **May 1, 1866**, Memphis Riot—46 killed
- **July 30, 1866**, New Orleans Massacre—238 killed
- **September 28, 1868**, Opelousas Massacre—approximately 150 killed
- **April 13, 1873**, Colfax Massacre—150 killed
- **September 4, 1875**, Clinton, Mississippi, Riot—50 killed
- **March 17, 1886**, Carroll County Courthouse Massacre—21 killed
- **November 23, 1887**, Thibodaux Massacre—60 killed

These further massacres are enumerated by the Zinn Education Project:[29]

- **December 7, 1874**, Vicksburg Massacre—as many as 300 killed
- **July 8, 1876**, Hamburg Massacre—6 killed
- **November 3, 1883**, Danville Riot—4 killed
- **August 5, 1896**, Polk County Massacre—3 killed
- **November 10, 1898**, Wilmington, North Carolina—at least 60 killed
- **August 14, 1908**, Springfield Massacre—6 killed
- **April 20, 1914**, Ludlow Massacre—13 killed
- **November 2, 1920**, Ocoee, Florida—more than 50 killed
- **September 15, 1963**, Birmingham, Alabama—4 girls killed and 14 injured
- **November 3, 1979**, Greensboro, North Carolina—5 killed
- **June 17, 2015**, Charleston, South Carolina—9 killed

The impact of this history of massacres, lynchings, and torture of African American people is not a thing of the past. Historian Leon F. Litwack writes,

The story of lynching is more than the simple fact of a Black man or woman hanged by the neck. It is a story of slow, methodical, sadistic, often highly inventive forms of torture and mutilation. Whether the victims were family members, friends, classmates, acquaintances, or strangers, African Americans who witnessed or heard about a lynching survived a deeply traumatic event and suffered a complex psychological harm.[30]

African American people are connected to this history and are consciously or unconsciously affected by it. White people are largely unaware of this history or may think it has no relevance today. So they may not see the connection to the Black Lives Matter movement and the continuing decisions by police commissioners, judges, and juries who fail to hold accountable the police officers who needlessly kill or abuse African American people.

AFRICAN AMERICAN PEOPLE KILLED BY POLICE 2014–2016

The following are fifteen African American people that we know of who were recently killed by police in little more than two years:

1. Eric Garner, July 17, 2014, New York City
2. Michael Brown, August 9, 2014, Ferguson, Missouri
3. Kajieme Powell, August 19, 2014, St. Louis, Missouri
4. Laquan McDonald, October 20, 2014, Chicago
5. Akai Gurley, November 20, 2014, Brooklyn
6. Tamir Rice, November 22, 2014, Cleveland, Ohio
7. Rumain Brisbon, December 22, 2014, Phoenix, Arizona
8. Tony Robinson, March 6, 2015, Madison, Wisconsin
9. Eric Harris, April 2, 2015, Tulsa, Oklahoma
10. Walter Scott, April 4, 2015, North Charleston, South Carolina
11. Freddy Gray, April 12, 2015, Baltimore, Maryland

12. Samuel DuBose, July 19, 2015, University of Cincinnati Police
13. Anton Sterling, July 5, 2016, Baton Rouge, Louisiana
14. Philando Castile, July 6, 2016, Falcon Heights, Minnesota
15. Terrence Crutcher, September 16, 2016, Tulsa, Oklahoma

At least 6,500 Black people were lynched from the end of the Civil War to 1950, an average of nearly two per week for nine decades. Nearly five Black people, on average, have been killed a week by law enforcement since 2015.[31]

Because of videos from police body cameras and, in one instance, cellphones, we also know of the deaths at the hands of police of Breonna Taylor on March 13, 2020, in Louisville, Kentucky; George Floyd on May 25, 2020, in Minnesota; and Rayshard Brooks on June 15, 2020, in Atlanta, Georgia. We also know that police kill more than two times as many African American people as white people despite the fact that African American people comprise only 13 percent of the U.S. population.[32]

Blessed are you when people revile you and persecute you and utter all kinds of evil against you falsely on my account.

—Matthew 5:11

A fundamental principle embraced by all religions is the Golden Rule of treating people the way you would like to be treated. Our dominant culture, made up of mostly white Christians, supported this horrific treatment of African American people. They were apparently blinded to the dichotomy between their "Christian values" and their support of this barbaric system. Likewise, today, many "Christian" people, unaware of their spiritual blindness, supported a blatantly racist president who continually stirred up racial tension, hatred, and fear of "others."

The Cross and the Lynching Tree

The cross has been transformed into a harmless, nonoffensive ornament that Christians wear around their necks. Rather than reminding us of the "costs of discipleship," it has become a form of "cheap grace," an easy way to salvation that doesn't force us to confront the power of Christ's message and mission. Until we can see the cross and the lynching tree together, until we can identify Christ with a "recrucified" Black body hanging from a lynching tree, there can be no genuine understanding of Christian identity in America, no deliverance from the brutal legacy of slavery and white supremacy.

—James H. Cone[33]

APPLICATION

Reflection

1. Consider when your ancestors arrived in the United States and their struggles with employment, access to education, as well as the impediments they had to overcome to gain a footing to begin to achieve the American Dream. How does it compare to the "impediments" of slavery, Jim Crow, the KKK, lynchings, and massacres?
2. Imagine how an African American person would feel upon reading this chapter and being reminded of this injustice suffered by her or his ancestors.
3. Imagine how you would feel after reading this chapter if your ancestors had been treated this way upon arriving in America.
4. Imagine how you would look upon those who have created these structures, institutions, and laws of oppression.

Discussion

1. Can you see a connection between instances of recent police brutality, which sparked the Black Lives Matter movement, and the history of police

standing by and permitting lynchings, massacres, and torture of African American people?

2. Can you understand why African American people may be reluctant to trust white people, police, and the judicial system?

3. Do you think you would feel the same about America if the people of your ethnicity had been and still were being treated as African American people were and are?

Response

1. Are you aware of any nonprofits that are fighting for civil rights of African American people today, such as the following ones?

- American Civil Liberties Union
- American Civil Rights Institute
- Black Action Movement
- Civil Liberty Defense Center
- Civil Rights Project of UCLA
- Congress of Racial Equality
- Equal Justice Under the Law
- National Association for the Advancement of Colored People
- Southern Poverty Law Center
- Student Non-Violent Coordinating Committee
- U.S. Commission on Civil Rights

2. Have you ever joined in any effort to overcome civil rights abuses by any group?

3. Do you have a desire to engage with others and fight for justice for any oppressed people?

4. Have you considered joining Black Lives Matter to advocate for justice?

5. Do you know of any ways you could volunteer to support the work of organizations fighting for justice for people whose civil rights are being violated today?

6. Would you be willing to work with others to research ways you could engage in efforts to support the civil rights of oppressed people?

Prayer Invitation

Abba, we beg you for the grace to see with the eyes of Jesus that all people, especially people of color, are made in your image and carry within them your Holy Spirit, your Son, Jesus.

Abba, help us to truly *see* each person we meet. Help us to understand the burden carried in the hearts of the ancestors of enslaved people. Help us to recognize ways we can use our gifts to respond to the injustices of racism.

---

* *Abba* is the Aramaic word used by Jesus to address God.

2

THE BACKLASH TO THE CIVIL RIGHTS MOVEMENT

God might have selected a rich, powerful nation as
his chosen people. Instead he chose oppressed slaves.
God picked an impoverished, enslaved people to be his
special instrument of revelation and salvation
to all people.

—Ronald Sider, *Rich Christians in an Age of Hunger:*
A Biblical Study

CONTROL THROUGH THE CRIMINAL JUSTICE SYSTEM

After slavery ended, every state in the South passed laws that
segregated, discriminated against, and controlled African
American people in every phase of life—choice of housing, jobs,
schools, churches, and restaurants, and access to restrooms,
drinking fountains, hotels, transportation, unions, military services, hospitals, orphanages, prisons, funeral homes, morgues,
and cemeteries. These were known as the Jim Crow[1] laws. The
"justification" for this type of social control was that African
Americans were treated "equally—but separately."

"IT SHALL BE UNLAWFUL for a negro and white person to play together or in company with each other in any game of cards or dice, dominoes, or checkers." (Birmingham, Alabama, 1930)

"IT SHALL BE UNLAWFUL for any white prisoner to be hand-cuffed or otherwise chained or tied to a negro prisoner." (Arkansas, 1903)

"No colored barber shall serve as a barber to a white woman or girls." (Atlanta, Georgia, 1926)

Jim Crow laws were blatantly illegal but were not success-fully challenged in our courts until 1954, when the Supreme Court in *Brown vs. The Board of Education of Topeka* found that treating African Americans "separately but equally" in education was unconstitutional. The facts in that case showed what should have been obvious for almost one hundred years and what is still obvious and true today: that African American children do not have access to the same educational resources as white children. This injustice in education was an acceptable fact to the white people in power before the *Brown* decision and is *still* acceptable in the United States today.

The *Brown* decision threatened the entire Jim Crow system and resulted in another backlash—a resurgence of the KKK as well as killings, bombings, and beatings of NAACP leaders who were working to combat racial injustice. Nevertheless, civil rights pro-tests continued to spring up all over. Between autumn of 1961 and spring of 1963, twenty thousand men, women, and children had been arrested in civil rights struggles.[2] John F. Kennedy announced the Civil Rights Bill. Lyndon B. Johnson passed the Civil Rights Act of 1964, which dismantled Jim Crow altogether. The Voting Rights Act of 1965 was passed. Reverend Martin Luther King Jr., along with many others, demanded a racial restructuring of soci-ety to address the needs of poor white and African Americans. So the backlash began.

MASS INCARCERATION

Just as lynchings, torture, massacres, and Jim Crow laws were a backlash to the end of slavery, there was also a backlash as a result of the civil rights movement of the 1950s and 1960s. A new system of control was created—the mass incarceration of African American people. Mass incarceration is a network of laws, policies, customs, and institutions that work to control African American people. This chapter will show how it was designed and implemented, and how it created a new racial caste system. The details of this system were researched and documented by Michelle Alexander in her widely acclaimed book *The New Jim Crow: Mass Incarceration in the Age of Colorblindness*, published in 2012.

Alexander reveals that ten years before writing her book, even she was not aware of the magnitude and severity of the backlash to the civil rights movement. She thought rising crime and incarceration rates were a function of poverty and the unequal education system. Through research, she learned there were powers that were consciously implementing a new racial caste system that was largely invisible to many African Americans and even to African American civil rights lawyers like herself: "Quite belatedly, I came to see mass incarceration…has emerged as a stunningly comprehensive, well-disguised system of radicalized social control that functioned in a manner strikingly similar to Jim Crow."[3]

If the establishment of this "new caste system" was invisible to her, how much more so would it be invisible to most white people? Many of the facts in this chapter come from her meticulous research. Information also comes from *Punishment without Crime* by Alexandra Natapoff, who reported on the magnitude and severity of the harm inflicted on African American people through the prosecution of misdemeanors.

> Remember those who are in prison, as though you were in prison with them; those who are being tortured, as though you yourselves were being tortured.
>
> —Hebrews 13:3

The United States has the highest rate of incarceration in the world—six to ten times greater than that of any other industrialized nation. In Germany, for example, 93 of every 100,000 adults are imprisoned. In the United States, there are 750 per 100,000. No other country in the world imprisons so many of its racial or ethnic minorities. The African American prison population went from around 300,000 to two million in less than thirty years.[4] The following are facts reported by Michelle Alexander:

- People of all races use and sell drugs at similar rates.[5] However, the rate of imprisonment of African American men versus white men for drug charges is significantly different. In some states, African American men have been admitted to prison on drug charges at rates twenty to fifty times greater than those of white men.[6]
- In the majority of cities, as many as 80 percent of young African American men now have criminal records and are thus subjected to legalized discrimination for the rest of their lives.[7]
- Three out of four young African American men in Washington, D.C. (nearly all of those in the poorest neighborhoods) can be expected to serve time in prison.[8] Similar rates of incarceration can be found in African American communities across America.

In poor African American neighborhoods today, almost every family has someone—son, daughter, father, mother, nephew, niece, aunt, or uncle—serving or who has served time in prison.

WHERE HAVE ALL THE AFRICAN AMERICAN MEN GONE?

They have been arrested and sent to prison. Since 1980, drug arrests have tripled to more than 31 million. In 1980, there were 41,000 in jail for drug offenses. Today, there are approximately half a million.[9] The only explanation for the sudden increase in the number of African American people in prison is the policy changes that targeted African Americans. These policies are a continuation of the historical methods of control of African American people by way of slavery, Jim Crow laws, Black Codes, convict labor, and so many other tactics of discrimination.

Do African Americans Use Drugs More than Whites?

- Studies show that **white youth are more likely** to engage in drug dealing than people of color.[10]
- Whites' use of cocaine is **seven times greater** than African Americans.[11]
- Whites' use of crack is **eight times greater** than African Americans.[12]
- Whites' use of heroin is **seven times greater** than African Americans.[13]
- White men ages twelve to seventeen were found to be admitted to emergency rooms for drug overdoses **three times more** than African Americans.[14]
- African Americans and whites use marijuana about the same.[15]

In spite of the above facts, the following are also true:

- While the majority of illegal drug users and dealers are white, 75 percent of all people in prison for drug offenses are African American or Latino.[16]
- African Americans were admitted to state prisons at rates thirteen times higher than whites.[17]
- Four in five convictions of African Americans were for drug use—not sales.[18]
- One in every fourteen African American men were in jail in 2006, compared to one in 106 white men.[19]
- In at least fifteen states, African Americans are admitted to prison on drug charges from twenty to fifty-seven times greater than that of white men.[20]

Are African Americans Punished More Severely than Whites?

- Crack, the drug most commonly used by African American people, is made from cocaine. Federal sentencing guidelines required sentences for crack to be **one hundred times more severe** than for powder cocaine used most frequently by white people.[21]
- African Americans were **six times more likely** to be sentenced as whites for the same crime.[22]
- Georgia has a "two strikes and you're out" policy. This means that two drug offenses will get you life in prison. The district attorney invoked "two strikes you're out" against whites 1 percent of the time and 60 percent of the time against Blacks. The result is that 98.4 percent of the people sentenced to life terms were Black.[23]

Today we are witnessing perhaps the greatest drug crime ever committed in U.S. history by drug manufacturers, distributors, and pharmacists, who made hundreds of millions of dollars by pushing and illegally distributing and selling opioid drugs. As the media shows images of young white people who have died because of overdoses, there is a greater understanding that drug addiction is a disease rather than a problem of law enforcement. The "war on crime" was a purely punitive approach to this disease. It focused primarily on African American people.

It might be hard for many white people to believe that powerful white people could be so evil as to deliberately inflict such cruelty on people because of their racial or ethnic identity. Could you imagine how you would feel if you were imprisoned or your daughter, son, mother, or father was targeted and imprisoned unfairly because they were white and suffering an addiction? This "New Jim Crow" began in the late sixties. It focused on "law and order." Tactics used to advocate for civil rights and equal treatment under the law, such as sit-ins, freedom rides, marches, boycotts, and other civil rights tactics, were characterized as criminal. The civil rights movement itself was considered a sign of a breakdown in law and order. Civil disobedience was seen as the leading crime. Segregationists used the sanitized rhetoric of "cracking down on crime." Richard Nixon called for a "war on drugs."[24]

Government officials designed and implemented strategies to take political advantage of the racism of voters. For example, H. R. Haldeman, one of President Nixon's key advisers, said, "He [Nixon] emphasized that you have to face the fact that the whole problem is really the Blacks. The key is to devise a system that recognizes this while not appearing to."[25]

Likewise, John Ehrlichman, special counsel to Nixon, explained the administration's campaign strategy of 1968 succinctly: "We'll go after the racists."[26] In Ehrlichman's view, "That subliminal appeal to the anti-Black voter was always present in Nixon's statements and speeches."[27] Republican strategist Kevin Phillips, who is often credited for offering the most influential argument in favor of a race-based strategy for Republican dominance of the South, argued in 1969 in *The Emerging Republican Majority* that Republicans would be successful if they continued to campaign primarily on the basis of racial issues, using coded anti-Black rhetoric.[28]

Ronald Reagan's strategy of racial hostility did not make explicit reference to race. He condemned "welfare queens" and "criminal predators." He had strong support among poor, white, working-class people. His "colorblind" rhetoric on crime, welfare, taxes, and state rights was understood by white voters. Reagan's racially coded rhetoric and strategy proved extremely effective, as 22 percent of all Democrats defected to vote for Reagan.[29] The use of racially coded rhetoric as well as very clear racist rhetoric and strategy continues most blatantly today in the speech of President Trump.

When crack cocaine appeared in 1985, the Reagan administration leaped at the opportunity to publicize crack cocaine to support the war on drugs.[30] The media published thousands of stories about Black crack prostitutes, crack babies, and gang bangers that reinforced prevalent stereotypes of Black women as irresponsible, selfish welfare queens and Black men as predators. Between October 1988 and October 1989, the *Washington Post* ran 1,565 stories about the "drug scourge."[31] The stage was set to implement the new system to control African Americans—the "new Jim Crow."

Growth of Prison Population

When the "war" began, federal budgets soared for law enforcement. Between 1980 and 1984, FBI funding increased from $8 million to $99 million. Department of Defense antidrug allocation increased from $33 million in 1981 to $142 million in 1991. During that same period, the Drug Enforcement Agency's antidrug spending grew from $86 million to $126 million, and FBI antidrug allocations grew from $38 million to $181 million.[32]

This war on drugs was a multimillion-dollar venture used to criminalize the poorest people of color, trapping them in a vicious cycle of addiction and incarceration. In the year 2000, the country spent almost $10 billion to incarcerate 500,000 non-violent drug offenders, 75 percent of whom were Black. In 2010 alone, the United States spent $27 billion for interdiction and law enforcement.[33]

Can you imagine how the lives of tens of thousands of African American people incarcerated for suffering an addiction could have been changed had our government used this $27 billion to provide economic support for addiction treatment programs and other preventive measures? The government wasn't trying to solve our drug addiction problem. The "war" was focused on punishing African American people who suffered addictions. Today, when it is clear that the opioid drug addiction problem affects many white people and their families, opioid drug addiction is seen as a public health issue rather than a law enforcement problem. Can you imagine how it would feel knowing your son or daughter, mother or father who is suffering an addiction is imprisoned and living among people with severe psychological problems and without access to mental health treatment while suffering an addiction?

The evidence that the war on drugs was a war on African American people can be clearly seen. It did not concentrate on campus fraternity houses or in the suburbs where illegal drugs were used by middle- and upper-class white people. It focused on poor African American communities. It resulted in untold suffering for virtually every African American family living in poor areas. In cities like Baltimore and Chicago, the vast majority of young men are under the control of the criminal justice system or branded criminals for life. This extraordinary circumstance—unheard of in the rest of the world—is treated here in America as a basic fact of life, as normal as separate water fountains were just a century ago.[34]

The children of imprisoned mothers and fathers also suffer this injustice. Since 1980, the number of incarcerated women has grown by more than 750 percent, a rate twice that of men. At least five million children—about 7 percent of American youth—have had an incarcerated parent, with Black, poor, and rural minorities disproportionately affected, according to a 2015 report that examined federal data. Studies show that the children face increasing risks of psychological and behavioral problems, insufficient sleep, and poor nutrition, as well as higher odds of entering the criminal justice system. The toll it takes on children is far more severe when the inmate is their mother. More than 60 percent of women in state prisons, and nearly 80 percent of those in jail, have minority children.[35]

White people who know of, accept, and overlook this injustice do so because of a spiritual blindness. They don't realize how their ignorance results in spiritual harm. So they see no need to respond to this injustice. Perhaps massive arrests simply reinforce the notion in their minds that a disproportionate number of African American people are indeed criminals. It reinforces the notion of white supremacy and the illusion that they are not like these criminals and are indeed superior to them. It also creates fear of African American men. It is a result of deliberate government strategies designed by politicians for their own self-interests.

> We have to recognize that there is a racial continuity between the killing fields of the plantations, the bodies hanging from the trees, police brutality, the prison industry, and the Superdome in New Orleans after Hurricane Katrina.
> —Cornell West, *Hope on a Tight Rope*

THE COSTS AFTER BEING ARRESTED

No other country in the world disenfranchises people who are released from prison in a manner even remotely resembling what happens in the United States. The United Nations Human Relations Committee has charged that the U.S. disenfranchisement policies are discriminatory and violate international laws.[36] Here are some of the ways the system is designed to maintain control of convicted persons after release from prison.

The convicted person—released without money, without a place to live, and with little chance of employment—can be denied welfare benefits, food stamps, the right to vote as well as federally funded education and federally funded healthcare. He or she will be required to indicate that he or she was a convict on job applications, rental agreements, loan applications, school applications, and so on.

The arrested person may be required to pay many agencies, including probation departments, courts, and child support enforcement officers. They can be charged for drug testing, drug treatment, per diem costs of pretrial detention, public defender application fees, and bail investigation fees. Post-conviction fees include presentence report fees, public defender recoupment fees, and fees levied on convicted persons placed in residential or work release programs. Many states pile on additional late fees, payment plan fees, and interest. Most ex-offenders can't pay these costs. When they work, their paychecks will be garnished. They can have up to 65 percent of wages garnished just for child support. And probation officers in most states can require 35 percent of the income of the ex-offender to pay for fines, fees, surcharges, and restitution charged by numerous agencies.[37] Many ex-offenders return to prison because they have not been able to pay these fines and fees and because they cannot find a decent job. Do you see how the deck is stacked to control African American people? Thousands of people with felony drug convictions are ineligible for food stamps for the rest of their lives, including pregnant women, people in drug treatment or recovering, and people suffering from AIDS.

How many white people are aware of the United Nations' charge that our treatment of African Americans violates international laws? Many white people believe that, regarding human rights, we are a beacon to the world and are different from other countries that oppress their people. Many aren't so good at seeing the log in their own eye.

> The LORD hears the needy,
> and does not despise his own that are in bonds.
>
> —Psalm 69:33

MISDEMEANORS

Misdemeanors include minor crimes such as disorderly conduct, jaywalking, loitering, spitting, marijuana possession, driving without a license, driving with a broken taillight, making an improper lane change, shoplifting ten dollars' worth of baby clothes, gambling, forging a check of less than twenty dollars, or speeding. Some misdemeanors are serious crimes, such as domestic violence and driving while intoxicated. There is overwhelming evidence that African American people are targeted and disproportionately arrested for misdemeanors. Every year, approximately thirteen million people are charged with misdemeanors. Conviction for a misdemeanor can be devastating for a family.

The punishment process for misdemeanors strips people of their liberty, money, health, jobs, housing, credit, immigration status, and government benefits.[38] Under federal law, a probation violation for any misdemeanor disqualifies an individual from welfare benefits, temporary assistance to needy families, food stamps, low-income housing, and supplemental security income for the elderly and disabled. The consequences of a drug misdemeanor conviction are particularly harsh and can include the loss of healthcare coverage, welfare, and student financial aid.[39]

Disproportionate African American Arrests

The following are only a few of the dozen examples of disproportionate arrests and punishment of African American people for misdemeanors:

- In Van Zandt County, Texas, approximately fifty miles from Dallas, Black people are thirty-four times more likely to be arrested for marijuana possession than white people.[40]
- In Iowa, Minnesota, and Illinois, African Americans are almost eight times more likely than whites to be arrested.[41]
- The Department of Justice found that in Ferguson, Missouri, where 67 percent of the population is African American, over 90 percent of the arrests and citations were of Black people.[42] They also found that, from 2011 to 2013, African Americans accounted for 95 percent of all Manner of Walking in Roadway charges and 94 percent of all Failure to Comply charges.[43]
- In Jacksonville, Florida, 55 percent of all pedestrian tickets are issued to African Americans, almost all of them in the city's poorest neighborhoods. Jacksonville is 29 percent Black.[44]
- In Urbana, Illinois, from 2007 to 2011, a full 91 percent of the people ticketed for jaywalking were Black, although only 16 percent of the residents are.[45]

All of the mothers and fathers, sons and daughters, spouses, grandmothers and grandfathers of people who are unjustly targeted, imprisoned, and controlled upon release suffer this injustice as well.

Just as surely as Black people suffer in a white society because they are Black, whites benefit because they are white....To go along with the racist institutions and structures such as the criminalized criminal justice system, to obviously accept the economic order as it is, and to just quietly go about your own personal business within institutional racism is to participate in white racism.

—Jim Wallis, *America's Original Sin*

APPLICATION

Catholic Social Teaching

"Responsibility, Rehabilitation, and Restoration," U.S. Conference of Catholic Bishops, 2000, no. 1:

> As Catholic Bishops, our response to crime in the United States is a moral test for our nation and a challenge for our church....Putting more people in prison and, sadly, more people to death, has not given Americans the security we seek. It is time for a new national dialogue on crime and corrections, justice and mercy, responsibility, and treatment. As Catholics, we need to ask the following: How can we restore a respect for law and life?

Reflection

1. Imagine how it would feel to be incarcerated on a drug charge, suffering an addiction, and living among some violent offenders and mentally ill people, without access to mental healthcare services.
2. Imagine your mother or father, son or daughter suffering an addiction and being imprisoned because she or he was targeted by police because of her or his ethnicity.
3. Imagine the heartbreak of millions of family members whose loved one suffering an addiction has

been targeted and imprisoned because of these tactics designed by powerful white people for their own political advantage.

Discussion

1. As you read of the injustices in this chapter, how did you feel?

   • Imagine how Jesus would feel about this injustice.
   • Imagine how you would feel if this injustice were done to you or a loved one.

2. How do you feel knowing that, in some states, African American men have been imprisoned on drug charges at rates twenty to fifty times greater than white men?[46]
3. Have you ever broken the law because of underage drinking, using marijuana, or traffic violations?
4. Were you ever treated disrespectfully by the police?
5. Have you or anyone in your family ever been confronted by a police officer for apparently breaking the law? What happened?
6. Was anyone that you know of ever abused by a police officer?
7. Do you think you or a family member should be incarcerated for using marijuana or committing other nonviolent misdemeanors? Why or why not?
8. Do you know of any white person ever arrested for a misdemeanor? What happened?
9. If you are arrested, would you have access to a lawyer and economic resources to keep you out of jail?
10. Has anyone in your extended family ever been arrested?

   • Did they have a lawyer?
   • Did they serve time?

Response

1. While reading of the injustice in this chapter, did you feel any "hunger" for justice?

   - Do you have a desire to advocate for reform of the criminal justice system?
   - Do you know the position of any of your congressional representatives at the state or federal level regarding reform of the criminal justice system?
   - Do you personally know of anyone who is engaged in efforts to reform the criminal justice system?
   - Would you be willing to pressure your congressional representatives to reform the criminal justice system?

2. Do you know of any organization that supports the families of imprisoned people?
3. Would you be willing to look into how you might volunteer to assist the spouse of a person imprisoned by services such as providing transportation for a visit or childcare?
4. Could you find out if, near you, there are lawyers who advocate for reform of the criminal justice system and ask if you could help?
5. Would you be willing to form a small group to research ways you could advocate for criminal justice reform?
6. Are there any ways you would be willing to respond to this injustice?

Prayer Invitation

Abba, help us to understand that in your kingdom there is no one that is least—none more precious than others. We beg you for the grace of understanding.

The Backlash to the Civil Rights Movement

Abba, gather into your heart all of the imprisoned and those harmed by the injustice of this system, and all their loved ones. *Abba*, embrace them, protect them, rescue them. Have mercy on them all.

Gather into your heart also all of those who have created and participated in this system so that, with the power of your love, they may be transformed and become instruments of mercy and justice.

Abba, ignite in our hearts the fire of your love so that by the power of your Holy Spirit, we will find ways to serve your will to bring about your kingdom of love and justice.

3

RESIDENTIAL SEGREGATION

What the eye doesn't see, the heart doesn't feel.

—Haitian proverb

It might seem that residential segregation came about because white and African American people have chosen to live in separate neighborhoods. In actuality, our neighborhoods have been *designed* by powerful white people to separate themselves from African American people. Our workplaces and churches, in large part, also keep us apart. So many white people don't get to see and interact with many African American people. If we don't get to be with people, we can't get to know them. If we don't know people, we can't relate to them. So when we read or hear of the harm African American people suffer due to racism, we might not care because we can't relate. Racial injustice has continued for centuries because it is easy for white people to turn a blind eye to the injustice of people they don't know.

In his book *The Color of Law: A Forgotten History of How Our Government Segregated America*, Richard Rothstein describes how residential segregation was *created* by government planning and laws and by the conscious tactics of banks, realtors, school boards, universities, and churches of various religions, and enforced by our courts and the police. Many of the facts presented in this chapter come from Rothstein's meticulous research.

Discrimination in housing has actually been illegal since 1866, when Congress passed the Civil Rights Act. It is also a violation of the Fourteenth Amendment regarding "equal treatment," as well as the Fair Housing Act of 1968. Nevertheless, our government has been permitting violations of the law for over 150 years.

According to the Department of Housing and Urban Development, each year there are an estimated two million complaints of housing discrimination made. The National Fair Housing Alliance estimates the number to be closer to four million per year. Each year millions of people complain of racial discrimination regarding housing issues, yet the federal government rarely takes one of these complaints to court. Between the years 1989 and 1992, only seventeen of these millions of complaints went to court nationwide.[1] The chance of a complaint of housing discrimination being found valid and prosecuted by the government is pretty slim. Our government has demonstrated little interest in enforcing the Fair Housing Act. Here are some examples of how our government has violated the law.

EXCLUSIONARY ZONING LAWS

Exclusionary zoning laws or ordinances prohibited African American people from buying homes on blocks where whites were a majority. In 1910, Baltimore was the first city to adopt an ordinance. Milton Dashiel, the lawyer who drafted Baltimore's ordinance, explained,

> Ordinarily, the Negro loves to gather to himself, for he is very gregarious and sociable in his nature. But those who have risen somewhat above their fellows appear to have an intense desire to leave them behind, disown them, as it were, and get as close to the company of white people as circumstances will permit them.[2]

Many other cities followed Baltimore by adopting exclusionary laws to keep African American people from getting close to white people: Atlanta, Birmingham, Dade County (Miami), Charleston, Dallas, Louisville, New Orleans, Oklahoma, Virginia, St. Louis, and others. These laws violated the Fourteenth Amendment and the Civil Rights Act of 1866. This "social engineering" was

45

designed by white people, mostly Christians, to keep white Christians away from African American people who are also mostly Christian.

REDLINING: FEDERAL HOUSING AUTHORITY'S DISCRIMINATORY PRACTICES

In 1933, as a result of the Great Depression, the government created the Home Owners' Loan Corporation (HOLC) to help people avoid eviction due to foreclosures.[3] The HOLC created color-coded maps of every metropolitan area of the country. There were red lines drawn around African American neighborhoods, representing areas that were considered high risk. African Americans were thus largely excluded from assistance through the HOLC.[4]

Another program to help with housing during the Great Depression was the Federal Housing Administration (FHA), which insured bank mortgages and made it easier for people to buy homes. Its appraisal standards included a **whites-only** requirement. That is, the FHA would not insure mortgages for African American people. So racial segregation was an official requirement of federal mortgage insurance programs.[5] The FHA also recommended—and, in many cases, demanded— that developers who received its construction loans for housing developments include **racially restrictive covenants** in their subdivisions' property deeds.[6] The FHA actually engineered segregation in housing. Here is how racially restricted covenants worked.

RESTRICTED COVENANTS

Restricted covenants were agreements in which government officials and developers agreed to restrict or prohibit African American families from living in white communities. Under these agreements, a neighbor could sue if an African American family made a purchase in one of these areas.[7] These agreements were common all over the country:

- From 1920 to 1932 in Philadelphia, the deeds of nearly four thousand houses included racially restricted covenants barring minorities from buying or living in a neighborhood. Being a "restricted section" was a major point for advertising. Northern cities used covenants amid the Great Migration of one million African American people. Racially restricted covenants were not made illegal until 1968.[8]
- A survey of three hundred developments in New York City built between 1935 and 1947 in Queens, Nassau, and West Chester Counties found that 56 percent had racially restrictive covenants.[9]
- By 1943, an estimated 175 Chicago neighborhood associations enforced deeds that barred sales or rentals to African Americans.[10]
- In Detroit from 1943 to 1965, white homeowners, real estate agents, or developers organized 192 associations to preserve racial exclusion. Cities and their suburbs in the west were also blanketed by racial covenants.[11]

Restricted Covenants by Churches and Universities

It was not just our government that used restricted covenants to keep white people from living near African American people. Churches, synagogues, and their clergy, as well as universities, professional associations, and insurance companies frequently led efforts to prevent African Americans from moving into white neighborhoods.[12] For example:

- In Los Angeles, the Reverend W. Clarence Wright, pastor of the fashionable Wilshire Presbyterian Church, led efforts to keep the Wilshire District all white. He personally sued to evict an African

American war veteran who had moved into a restricted area in 1947.[13]

- On Chicago's South Side, signatures of a 1928 restrictive covenant were obtained in door-to-door solicitations by the priest of St. Anselm Catholic Church, the rabbi of Congregation Beth Jacob, and the executive director of the area's property owners' association. Trinity Congregational Church was also party to the agreement.[14]
- The University of Chicago organized and guided property owners' associations that were devoted to preventing African American families from moving nearby.[15]
- Insurance companies also participated in segregation. Metropolitan Life developed a project, a nine-thousand-unit Stuyvesant Town housing complex on the East Side of Manhattan. The project was for "white people only."[16]
- State Real Estate Commissions denied licenses to brokers who sold African Americans homes in white neighborhoods.[17]

SEGREGATION CREATED BY THE 1949 HOUSING ACT

In 1949, the Housing Act was passed in response to the severe shortage of housing for veterans returning from the war. The Housing Act permitted local authorities to continue to design *separate* public housing projects for African Americans and whites and to *segregate* African Americans and whites within the projects.[18]

In 1984, reporters from the *Dallas Morning News* visited federally funded developments in forty-seven metropolitan areas. They found that nearly ten million public housing tenants were almost always segregated by race, and all of the white projects had facilities, amenities, services, and maintenance superior to those found in predominantly Black projects. The federal courts in Chicago, Baltimore, Dallas, San Francisco, Miami, Yonkers, and other places recognized that Housing and Urban Development and local governments had *created and perpetuated segregation*.[19]

Our government consciously and purposefully designed public housing to keep African American people away from white people and to underfund the services and maintenance of African American housing. Even if the white people who designed these policies did not "intend" to harm African American people, they nevertheless did so. Collectively, they just designed the systems that resulted in African American and white people living separate lives. It has resulted in the lack of interaction and understanding that exists today between white people and African American people.

BLOCKBUSTING

White flight was not an accident—it was a triumph of racist social engineering.

—Ta-Nehisi Coates, *The Case for Reparations*

Blockbusting is a scheme in which speculators bought properties in borderline African American and white areas. They rented or sold them to African American families at above-market prices. They then persuaded white families in these areas that their neighborhoods were turning into African American slums and that values would soon fall precipitously. They purchased the homes of the panicked white people for less than they were worth and sold them to African American people at inflated prices.[20]

Their tactics included hiring African American women to push baby carriages through white neighborhoods, hiring African American men to drive cars with radios blasting through white neighborhoods, paying African American men to accompany agents knocking on doors to see if homes were for sale, making random telephone calls to residents in white neighborhoods and asking to speak to someone with a stereotypical African American name like Johnnie Mae.[21]

These diabolical tactics worked because of white people's

fear of African American people. This fear is the result of a lack of understanding of African American people that has resulted from more than four hundred years of segregation created by powerful white people.

Another example of efforts to harm and take economic advantage of African American people was reported in an article published in 1962 in the *Saturday Evening Post*. An agent using the pseudonym Norris Vitchek claimed to have arranged house burglaries in white communities to scare neighbors into believing that their communities were becoming unsafe. Fear caused home sales to increase. Real estate firms then sold the newly acquired properties at inflated prices to African American people. Because most African American families could not qualify for mortgages under FHA and bank policies, the agents often sold these homes on installment plans known as "contract sales." These agreements usually provided that ownerships would transfer to purchasers after fifteen or twenty years, but if a *single monthly payment were late*, the owner-speculator could evict the would-be owner who had accumulated no equity. The inflated sale price made it all the more likely that payment would not be on time. Owners-speculators could then resell these homes to new contract buyers.[22] Chapter 8 will consider the tremendous loss of wealth of African American families because of tactics like these, which prevented African American families from accumulating wealth from the increased equity that normally results from increasing real estate values.

RESIDENTIAL SEGREGATION ENFORCED BY VIOLENCE

The following are just a very few instances of violence being used to keep African American people from living near white people:

From 1917 to 1921, when Chicago was first being rigidly defined, there were fifty-eight fire bombings of homes in white border areas to which African Americans had moved, with no arrests or prosecutions—despite the deaths of two African American residents.[23] How many times have we heard of African American people being killed needlessly by police who are then not tried or convicted? The lack of regard for the safety of African American people continues to this day.

In the first five years after World War II, 357 reported "incidents" of violence were directed against African Americans attempting to rent or buy in Chicago's racial border areas.[24]

In Los Angeles in 1945, a family (mother, father, and two children) was killed when their new home in an all-white neighborhood was blown up. Of the more than one hundred incidents of move-in bombings and vandalism that occurred in Los Angeles between 1950 and 1965, only one led to an arrest and prosecution.[25]

In 1954, when Andrew Wade, an African American electrical contractor and Korean War Navy veteran, purchased a home in a middle-class African American neighborhood in Louisville, Kentucky, a crowd gathered in front and a cross was burned on an empty lot next door. On the first night, rocks crashed through the front window with a message, "Nigger, get out." Ten rifle shots were fired through the kitchen door. Under the watch of a police guard, demonstrations continued for a month until the house was dynamited. None of the perpetrators were arrested.[26]

In the late 1950s, white homeowners wanting to leave Levittown, Pennsylvania, realized that it would be to their benefit to sell to African Americans who, because they were desperate for housing, would pay more than whites. In 1957, an African American veteran, Bill Meyers, and his wife, Daisy, found a Levittown homeowner willing to sell. Meyers had served in World War II. He was discharged as a staff sergeant. Daisy Meyers was a college graduate. No bank would provide a mortgage because they were African American. However,

51

a New York City philanthropist gave them a private mortgage.[27]

After Bill and Daisy bought their home, a mail carrier making his rounds shouted, "Niggers have moved into Levittown." Six hundred demonstrators then assembled in front of the house and pelted it with rocks. Some rented a unit next door and set up a clubhouse from which a confederate flag flew and music blared all night. The police arrived but were ineffective. For two months, police stood by as rocks were thrown, crosses were burned, the KKK symbol was painted on the walls of the clubhouse next door, and the house was vandalized. Some police officers were assigned to protect the family but rather than doing so, they stood by with the mob, joking and encouraging the participants.[28] Finally, Bill and Daisy Meyers were forced to leave.

HOW THE SHARKS TOOK ADVANTAGE OF THE HUD ACT OF 1968

In the sixties, there were urban uprisings in many cities, including Philadelphia, Harlem, Watts, Newark, Detroit, Chicago, Washington, and Baltimore. A major cause according to the Kerner Commission Report was government-sponsored housing segregation that confined African American people to rental houses in urban areas. African American people wanted to enjoy homeownership. So the government responded with the passage of the Housing and Urban Development (HUD) Act of 1968. It created a policy to enable low-income Black renters to become homeowners by providing the following support:

- down payment of two hundred dollars
- linking the mortgage to income—not the value of the home
- capping the interest rate at 1 percent

The following is a summary of "When Owning a Home Is a Nightmare," published in the *New York Times* on October 20, 2019, prior to the publication of *Race for Profit*, written by Keeanga-Yamahtta Taylor, assistant professor of African American studies at Princeton.

In response to the HUD Act, speculators bought decrepit or even condemned houses cheaply and quickly flipped them. Federal Housing Authority appraisers would sometimes take bribes and inflate the values of the homes. Thousands of poor African American women were recruited to be homeowners because they were more likely to fall behind on their payments. With foreclosure, the banks could profit from being repaid for inflated mortgages and profit again when the foreclosed property was resold to another poor family that qualified for a government-guaranteed mortgage.

The banks made money on both the fee to make the loan and on the closing costs to sell the house. They cared only about issuing a large number of mortgages that they would package and resell. It didn't matter if the house went into foreclosure—they would make their money because the government paid the mortgage of the foreclosed home. As a result, the nation's first program to encourage Black ownership ended in the 1980s with *tens of thousands* of foreclosures. It was a gold mine for the real estate agents and mortgage lenders. The indiscriminate FHA lending that resulted in tens of thousands of foreclosures perpetuated the perception of Black neighborhoods as dilapidated and deteriorating. Our failure to fully recognize this history has meant that housing policy today continues to revolve around market-based solutions even as Black ownership rates fall to historic lows.

DISCRIMINATION IN HOUSING TODAY

In 2015 and 2016, African Americans were **ten times** less likely than white people to receive conventional mortgage loans.[29] In an analysis of this issue, the Center of Investigative Reporting showed that African American and Latin American loan applications were more likely to be denied than those of white applicants in the same neighborhoods, even when income and other factors were comparable. Data showed that Black applicants were turned away at slightly higher rates than whites in forty-eight cities. Latin American applicants were more likely to be turned away in twenty-five cities. The practice of redlining is alive and well today.

Today, the percentage of African American people who own their own homes is falling. Reporter Troy McMullen found that in 2004, nearly half of all African American families owned a home. It fell to 43 percent in 2017, virtually erasing all the gains made by the passage of the Fair Housing Act in 1968, despite a strengthening economy as well as record low unemployment and higher wages for Black workers. It has dropped incrementally almost every year since 2014 for African American people.[30]

McMullen reported that researchers at the Urban Institute found large disparities between the homeownership rate of Black families and white families in all one hundred of the cities with the largest Black populations, pushing the housing gap between the two groups to its highest in more than fifty years. Discrimination played a role in creating that gap. A study by the National Fair Housing Alliance found that real estate discrimination was pervasive in at least a dozen major metropolitan areas, including the District of Columbia. African American testers posing as homebuyers were often denied information about special incentives that would have made the purchase easier and required to produce loan pre-approval letters and other documents when whites were not.

Securing a mortgage is more challenging for African Americans. McMullen reported that, according to the Federal Consumer Financial Protection Bureau in 2017, 19.3 percent of Black applicants were denied a conventional home loan, compared with 7.9 percent of whites. The refinancing market saw similar differentials with Blacks rejected on 39 percent of their applications and whites on 22.9 percent.

THE BEAT GOES ON

The first significant federal intervention to expand housing opportunities for African American people since the Civil Rights Act of 1968 was the passage of the Affirmatively Furthering Fair House Rule by the Obama administration in 2015. It required municipalities seeking federal grants to develop plans to overcome barriers to racial and economic integration. It was repealed by Trump. He tweeted in July, "I am happy to inform all of the people living their 'Suburban Lifestyle Dream' that you will no longer be bothered or financially hurt by having low income housing built in your neighborhood. Your housing prices will go up based on the market, and crime will go down."

Trump was interviewed in July by *Fox News* host Laura Ingraham. He told her, "They are trying to destroy the suburban, beautiful—the American dream, really. They want low income housing, and with that comes a lot of other problems, including crime. It's not nice to say, but I'll say it."[31]

Residential segregation is one important component of the web of injustice created to control African American people. It resulted in segregation in education since children attend schools in their neighborhood. As you will see in chapter 8, it created significant disparities in wealth. It also resulted in the environmental racism discussed in chapter 6. It is all connected, insidious, and deeply harmful. It is structural injustice that results in institutionalized violence.

It is easy for white people who live in isolation of African American people to be unaware of how this structural injustice affects African American people, because they don't get to see and know many African American people. So they don't know how it causes harm and are unaware of their own spiritual blindness. This blindness perpetuates the injustice, as they see no need to respond. It is simply accepted. They are unaware of the moral injury that they suffer.

APPLICATION

Catholic Social Teaching

Racism is a sin that divides the human family, blots out the image of God among specific members of that family, and violates the fundamental dignity of those called to be children of the same Father. Racism is the sin that says some human beings are inherently superior and others essentially inferior because of races. It is the sin that makes racial characteristics the determining factor for the exercise of human rights. It mocks the words of Jesus: "Treat others the way you would have them treat you." Indeed, racism is more than a disregard for the words of Jesus; it is a denial of the truth of the dignity of each human being revealed by the mystery of the incarnation.[32]

Reflection & Discussion

1. Have you ever walked or driven through an impoverished African American community? If so, what was your reaction?

    - Imagine Jesus's reaction after walking through an impoverished African American neighborhood and then walking through an upper-middle-class white neighborhood.
    - Imagine how your understanding of African American people today would be different if your grandparents, parents, and you grew up in integrated communities, attended the same schools, worked with and worshiped in the same churches as African American people and other people of color.
    - Imagine how your life would be different today if, for generations, your family lived in integrated communities and had many African American friends involved in all of your lives.

2. Can you think of any harm or loss you have suffered as a result of being isolated from African American people and their culture?
3. Can you think of the ways that you have benefited by living in your neighborhood rather than an impoverished African American neighborhood?

Response

1. Do you have a desire to get to know African American people better?
2. Can you think of anything you could do to get a better understanding of African American people who live in or near your community?

   - Is there an African American museum in your city?
   - Have you ever driven through the most impoverished African American neighborhood near you?
   - Is there an elderly African American person whom you know that you could talk to, to give you an insight into what it was like living with Jim Crow laws?
   - Would you consider visiting or worshiping at an African American church in a nearby community?

3. Would you consider volunteering to serve in a predominantly African American school to tutor or to read to children?
4. Would you be willing to consider volunteering to help with the needs of the elderly or people "shut in" living in an African American community?
5. Has your church ever reached out to connect with African American churches or communities?
6. Can you think of ways that your church members could reach out to get to know and get involved in

some way to understand and serve the needs of impoverished people of color?

Prayer Invitation

Abba, grant us a grateful heart and mindfulness of the gift of being raised in a safe community with access to good schools, supermarkets, and playgrounds.

Grant us the grace to be mindful of our neighbors who live in dangerous places in fear of harm from gun violence and industrial toxins. Ignite in our hearts the fire of your Holy Spirit so that we find the wisdom and courage to be a voice against the forces that divide and separate your people. Grant us opportunities to get to meet and know all of our sisters and brothers, especially those who suffer the injustice of racism.

4

SEGREGATION IN EDUCATION

The educational deck has been consciously, systematically, and intentionally stacked in favor of middle- and upper-middle-class white children and against African American children for our entire history. These injustices, like the injustices in housing, have been embedded in our laws, implemented through government policies, and upheld by our courts—that is, our legislative, executive, and judicial branches.

Racial segregation by government action violates the Constitution and the Bill of Rights as well as the Fifth, Thirteenth, and Fourteenth Amendments. However, our courts did not address the unconstitutional practice of school segregation until 1954 in *Brown vs. The Board of Education of Topeka* when the Supreme Court decided that segregated schools did not provide African American students with an education that was "equal" to that of white students.

Imagine! It took from 1868 until 1954 for our courts to recognize what should have been clear to everyone: our segregated African American schools were not equal to our white schools. They are not equal today. The disparity was much greater before *Brown*. But even after the *Brown* decision in 1954, it took until the passage of the Civil Rights Act in 1964 for the government to begin to enforce desegregation in schools. Then there was a backlash.

From 1970 to 1990, steady progress was made in school desegregation. According to a report of the UCLA Project on Civil Rights, by 1988, the percentage of African American students in white schools in the South rose from nearly zero to 43.5 percent. But it did not take long for the courts to begin to make rulings that began to *reverse* these gains. By 2011, that figure was 23.2 percent, just *below* where it stood in 1970. From 1970 to 2011, any progress made to desegregate schools in the South was lost.[1] The losses began after a decision in 1977 by Judge Luther Bohanon in Oklahoma.

In 1972, as a result of a lawsuit filed by an African American optometrist, A. L. Dowell, Oklahoma City was forced by Judge Luther Bohanon to develop a plan to desegregate its schools. It implemented a busing plan and achieved some degree of integration. In 1977, however, Judge Bohanon ruled that because the city had been declared in compliance with its desegregation plan, it could be *released* from the order to desegregate. In other words, the judge ruled that because Oklahoma City achieved some degree of desegregation, it was permitted to *discontinue* using the methods it used to desegregate.[2] Not surprisingly, when the plans and the methods that caused integration were eliminated, segregation began again. Judges are not naïve. Judge Bohanon had to know what would happen when the plans and methods used to cause integration were eliminated. It is simple logic. That case set a precedent, which allowed school districts around the country to be *released* from desegregation orders if they could prove they had successfully integrated their public schools.

In 2007, another Supreme Court decision, *Parents Involved in Community Schools vs. Seattle School District No. 1*, struck down a voluntary desegregation plan in Seattle.[3] The court said that the means that the school districts used to voluntarily desegregate were unconstitutional because the means to desegregate "*took race into account.*" How could a plan to reverse segregation not "take race into account"?

The Civil Rights Project reported on this decision in August 2007:

> The court's basic conclusion, that it was unconstitutional to take race into account in order to end segregation, represents a dramatic reversal of the ruling of the civil rights era, which held that race *must* (emphasis added) be taken into account to the extent necessary to end racial separation.
>
> The Supreme Court reversed nearly four decades of progress. It rejected the conclusion of several major

social science briefs submitted by researchers and professional associations which reported that such policies would foster increased segregation in schools that were systematically unequal and undermine educational opportunities for both minorities and white students.[4]

The Supreme Court justices of the highest court in America must have known of the consequences that would result from their decision. Resegregation was engineered by the Supreme Court. These were not unconscious decisions.

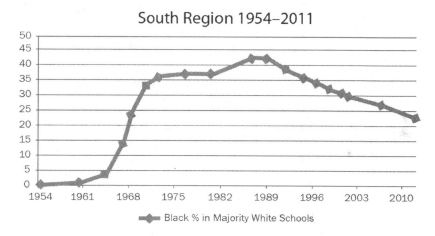

South Region 1954–2011

Black % in Majority White Schools

Figure 2: Southern Desegregation and Resegregation for Black Students, 1954–2011[5]

Researchers reporting in the *Journal of Policy and Analysis Management* found that almost half of the school districts that were under court order to desegregate as of 1990 had been released from court oversight in the last two decades. The rate at which districts have been released has increased over time. More than twice as many districts were released in the 2000s as in the 1900s. The *Journal* reported that if these trends continue, the era of federal supervision of school segregation that began with the *Brown* decision will soon be at an end.[6]

An example of continuing efforts to segregate public schools is the recent agreement between the Sausalito Marin City School

District and the California attorney general to desegregate schools by the 2020/21 school year. After two years of investigation, the state's attorney general found the school district had "knowingly and intentionally maintained and exacerbated" racial segregation and even established an intentionally segregated school. California Attorney General Xavier Becerra said that the arrangement was no accident. It was a deliberate scheme by the school district to set up a separate and unequal system that would keep low-income children of color out of a white school. "Depriving a child of a fair chance to learn is wicked, it's warped, it's morally bankrupt, and it's corrupt," Mr. Becerra said. "Your skin color or zip code should not determine winners and losers." The State of California said the district violated the Equal Protection Clause of the California Constitution. Sixty-five years after *Brown vs. the Board of Education*, California, New York, Maryland, Illinois, and other liberal states have the most deeply segregated schools in our nation.[7]

WHITES HAVE THE LEAST EXPOSURE TO STUDENTS OF OTHER RACES

Segregation in education deprives both white students and students of color of learning opportunities. Racially and ethnically diverse classrooms benefit all students. What we learn and how we learn are shaped by with whom we interact and the context of those interactions. Diverse learning opportunities enrich the content of what we learn and also our abilities to learn. The greater success we have in learning how to learn from and with people who bring different perspectives to a situation, the more powerful will be our abilities to understand and to reason. Getting to know the personal histories of people who are different from us, who do not share our racial and ethnic backgrounds, breaks down stereotypes. Eliminating stereotypes increases our learning opportunities and our cognitive capabilities.[8]

UCLA researchers found that white children have the least exposure to students of other races. Today's typical white student attends a school that is nearly 75 percent white, but only one-eighth Latin American and one-twelfth African American. Put another way, in a classroom of thirty students, the average white student has twenty-one white classmates, two African American classmates, four Latin Americans, one Asian, and one "other." Conversely, the typical African American or Latin American student would have eight white classmates and at least twenty minority classmates of color.

The fate of African American and white students is linked. Both can benefit by knowing and working together. Both are deprived of learning opportunities because of segregation. Besides the educational harm, white people are harmed spiritually by not knowing, understanding, and caring for people who suffer injustice created by the organizations that were designed to benefit them and not others. They are beneficiaries of an unjust educational system. This systematic injustice also includes African American students suffering sickness because of environmental hazards in their schools.

TOXIC SCHOOLS

Children from low-income families are also at risk of suffering from exposures to asbestos fibers, lead dust, and other environmental hazards in their schools. As part of its Toxic City series, the *Philadelphia Inquirer* and *Daily News* investigated the physical conditions at Philadelphia district-run schools.[9] At least three-quarters of children in Philadelphia district schools are from low-income families. Sixty-five percent are minorities. Reporters examined five years of internal maintenance logs and building records, and interviewed 120 teachers, nurses, parents, students, and experts. They identified more than nine thousand environmental problems related to filthy schools and unsafe conditions, including mold, deteriorated asbestos, and acres of flaking and peeling paint likely to contain lead.

The district's records reportedly revealed the following: backed-up sewage; leaking radiators; mice droppings along chalkboard ledges and inside plastic lunch storage bins; mold in bathrooms, closets, and classrooms; thirty-four reports of flaking paint; twenty-nine reports of damaged asbestos; ninety-five reports of asthma triggers such as mold, mice droppings, and cockroaches. The list goes on. Children told of shivering in class-rooms without heat and having to wear winter coats to keep warm. They wrote of regularly seeing rats and mice in the lunch-room. "Every day I go to school, I feel like I'm in a prison or a junkyard," student Chelsea Mungo, then aged ten, wrote in a letter to her state senator, Vincent Hughes (D, Philadelphia).

Lead Exposure

Of fourteen elementary schools tested by the newspapers, ten had unsafe levels of toxic residue from flaking lead paint on windowsills, shelves, or classroom floors. A significant route of lead entry into a child's blood is through hand-to-mouth con-tact leading to ingestion of lead dust. Children living in poverty tend to have poor nutrition, making it easier for the lead to be absorbed into the body. Once absorbed into the body, it stays for life. Lead in a child's blood can cause decreased intelligence, impaired neurobehavioral development, brain and nervous sys-tem disorders, decreased stature, and anemia.

Asbestos Exposure

Asbestos dust is a carcinogen known to cause several types of cancer. Dangerous exposure exists when fibers become airborne and are breathed. When the Philadelphia school dis-trict did its last full inspection in the 2015/16 school year, more than 80 percent of the schools had damaged asbestos. Gouged, cracked, or loose asbestos was found in 2,252 locations, includ-ing many frequented by children. In more than one-quarter, or 639 locations, the district's environmental inspectors were so concerned that they marked the damaged spots as "high pri-ority" and "newly friable" because of the potential health risk. "Friable" refers to asbestos that, when dry, may be crumbled, pulverized, or reduced to powder by hand pressure. It can then become airborne and breathed in by the children.

Philadelphia Inquirer reporters collected dust samples on eighty-four surfaces in eleven Philadelphia district schools. Nine of the eleven schools had elevated asbestos fiber counts in student-accessible areas. Half of the samples were above five thousand fibers per square centimeter, the level the EPA set to qualify for federal cleanup of apartments near Ground Zero after 9/11.

In the 2015/16 school year, inspectors noted 960 locations with damaged asbestos floor tile, totaling roughly 12,300 square feet. Damaged asbestos floor tile can result in the liberation of asbestos fibers that the children can breathe.

ARE PHILADELPHIA SCHOOLS AN ANOMALY?

Research shows that Philadelphia schools are not an anomaly. Best Educational Success Together (BEST) is a collaborative of organizations engaged in educational reform and social justice. It reported on research related to deteriorating public schools in its publication, "Growth and Disparity—A Decade of U.S. Public School Construction."[10] BEST found that the most academically needy students—minority and impoverished students—were most likely to attend the most decrepit facilities. The analysis looked at the decade from 1995 through 2004, the most current information available. During that time, there was unprecedented spending and growth in school facility construction across the nation. Over this decade, more than two thousand new schools were built and more than 130,000 were renovated and had other improvement projects to address health and safety technology, access for students with disability, educational enhancement, and other needs. The report found that the billions of dollars spent on facilities were not equally available to affluent and low-income communities and for minority and white students:

- The least affluent school districts made the lowest investment ($4,800 per student) while the most affluent districts made the highest investment ($9,361 per student).[11]
- Money spent on schools serving low-income students was more likely to fund basic repairs such as new roofs and asbestos removal, while schools in

more affluent districts were more likely to receive
funds for educational enhancements such as
science labs or performing arts centers.[12]

- The lowest investment ($4,140 per student) was
  made in the poorest communities, while the
  highest investment ($11,500 per student) was made
  in the high-income communities.[13]
- School districts with predominantly students
  of color enrolled invested the least ($5,172 per
  student), while school districts with predominantly
  white students enrolled spent the most ($7,102 per
  student).[14]

This disproportionate spending is another example of
structural injustice, that is, decisions made by the powerful to
systematically spend more money to enhance the educational
opportunities of relatively high-income children (mostly white
people) and to spend less on lower-income children (mostly
minority children). The report indicated that an increasing body
of research shows that poor building conditions, such as lack of
temperature control, poor indoor air quality, insufficient daylight, overcrowded classrooms, and lack of specialty classrooms
are obstacles to academic achievement.[15]

Research confirms what many educators already know.
When school facilities are clean, in good repair, and designed
to support high academic standards, there will be higher student achievement, independent of student socioeconomic status.
There is growing evidence to support these findings:

- The cognitive requirements for learning and
  teaching—motivation, energy, attention, hearing,
  and seeing—are affected by the physical
  surroundings where they take place.[16]
- There is a positive relationship between a school's
  compliance with health and safety regulations and
  its academic performance.[17]
- The amount of natural light, the indoor air quality,
  the temperature, and the cleanliness of schools and
  classrooms all impact student learning.[18]

- Overcrowded schools lead to higher absenteeism rates for both students and teachers and have detrimental effects on a children's ability to learn and perform well.[19]
- Poor building conditions greatly increase the likelihood that teachers will leave their school, a troubling fact given the need for more and better teachers in most disadvantaged schools.[20]
- School facility quality is an important predictor that teachers will leave their current position.[21]
- Poor facility conditions make it more difficult for teachers to deliver an adequate education to their students and adversely affect teachers' health.[22]

INEQUALITIES IN TEACHING AND RESOURCES

The U.S. educational system is one of the most unequal in the industrialized world. Students routinely receive dramatically different learning opportunities based on their social status. Linda Darling-Hammond of Stanford University's School of Education reports on the inequalities in teaching and resources given to African American students in a report entitled "Inequality in Teaching and Schooling: How Opportunity Is Rationed to Students of Color in America."[23] She notes the following:

- The wealthiest 10 percent of school districts in the United States spend nearly **ten times** more than the poorest 10 percent.
- Minority students have fewer and lower-quality books, curriculum materials, laboratories, and computers; significantly larger class sizes; less qualified and experienced teachers; and less access to high-quality curriculum.
- African American students are nearly twice as likely to be assigned to the most ineffective teachers and about half as likely to be assigned to the most effective teachers.

- Minority and low-income students in urban settings are most likely to find themselves in classrooms staffed by inadequately prepared, inexperienced, ill-qualified teachers because funding inequities, distribution of local power, labor market conditions, and dysfunctional hiring practices conspire to produce teacher shortages of which they bear the brunt.

If our schools were indeed integrated, we would not have these disparities.

CORPORAL PUNISHMENT OF AFRICAN AMERICAN CHILDREN

There are more than three times as many white children in U.S. public schools,[24] yet African American children are twice as likely to be subjected to corporal punishment than white children. People who have been hurt are more likely to hurt others. In their anger from being physically abused, children may try to take their pain out on other children. They may also develop a lifetime habit of using violence to defend themselves.

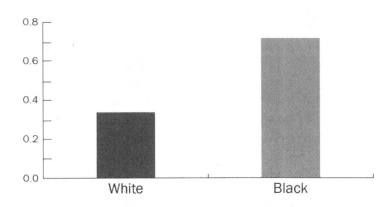

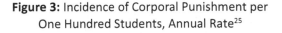

Figure 3: Incidence of Corporal Punishment per One Hundred Students, Annual Rate[25]

Disproportionate Discipline

African American students are no more likely to misbehave than any other students from the same social and economic environments.[26] Yet, the UCLA Civil Rights Project found that African American students were three times as likely as their peers to be issued out-of-school suspensions, along with nearly one in thirteen Latin American students.[27] In New Jersey public schools, on average, African American students were found to be almost **sixty times** as likely as white students to be expelled for serious disciplinary infractions.[28]

School-to-Prison Pipeline

Studies also show that a history of school suspensions or expulsions is a strong predictor of future trouble with the law—and the first step on what civil rights leaders have described as a "school-to-prison pipeline" for African American youth. The American Civil Liberties Union has this to say about school suspensions:

> Suspensions, often the first stop along the pipeline, play a crucial role in punishing students from the school system and into the criminal justice system. Research shows a clear correlation between suspensions and both low achievement and dropping out of school altogether. Such research also demonstrates a link between dropping out of school and incarceration later in life. Specifically, students who have been suspended are three times more likely to drop out by the tenth grade than students who have never been suspended. Dropping out in turn triples the likelihood that a person will be incarcerated later in life. In 1997, 68 percent of prison inmates were school dropouts.[29]

With our schools having three times as many white students as African American students, all things being equal, we would expect white students to be suspended, expelled, and referred to law enforcement three times as frequently as African American students. However, that is not the case.

	White	African-American	Hispanic	Asian/Pacific Islander	American Indian
Percentage of school population	51%	18%	24%	6%	1%
In-school suspension	39%	35%	23%	6%	1%
Out-of-school suspension (single)	36%	35%	25%	3%	1%
Out-of-school suspension (multiple)	29%	46%	22%	1%	1%
Expulsion	33%	39%	24%	2%	1%
Referral to law enforcement	25%	42%	29%	3%	1%

Figure 4: Disparities in School Discipline[30]

Disparities in school discipline were also reported by the U.S. Department of Education Office of Civil Rights. It found the following:[31]

- Black preschool children were 3.6 times as likely to receive one or more out-of-school suspensions than white preschool children.
- Black K–12 students are 3.8 times as likely to receive one or more out-of-school suspensions than white students.
- Black students are 1.9 times as likely to be expelled from school without education services as white students.
- Black students are more likely to be disciplined through law enforcement: Black students are two and a half times as likely to receive a referral to law enforcement or be subjected to a school-related arrest as white students.

This unjust, disproportionate treatment of African American children in education has been a violation of our Constitution for over 150 years. Despite the research that shows this mistreatment and despite many lawsuits, it persists. Access to a good education is perhaps the greatest hope for many African American children. However, those in power have continually designed systems of funding that give greater opportunity to white children at the expense of African American children. The fact that African American children are being physically abused is simply appalling.

APPLICATION

Catholic Social Teaching

Virtually every social challenge facing the United States—education, care for the environment, access to healthcare, poverty, capital punishment, immigration reform, workers' rights, HIV/AIDS, criminal justice, right to life, concern for women—is entangled with or aggravated by racial bias against people of color. We cannot have an honest engagement with racial injustice without addressing the unequal social status that results from it and the reasons for it. We are all wounded by the sin of racism; yet most Americans lack an adequate understanding of its depths, extent, and true nature.[32]

Reflection

1. Imagine Jesus, who turned over the tables of the money changers at the temple, turning over the tables of the politicians who have stacked the deck against African American children.
2. Imagine how things would be different in America if, for the last 150 years, African American children had the same education as white children:

   • Many more university-educated African American people would have qualified for jobs requiring a university degree if they would have had equal access to educational opportunities.

- Our society would have experienced untold changes for the better had there been more university-educated African American people employed as lawyers and doctors and in positions of power in corporations, unions, universities, elected positions, and government administration for the last 150 years.

3. Imagine the countless dreams of generations of African American people that have been denied by powerful white people who limited African American children's educational opportunities while providing adequate support for white children.

Discussion

1. Did you know the extent of the injustice in education before reading this chapter? If not, do you know why not?
2. Did you feel a hunger for justice or a sense of outrage as you read this chapter?
3. Aren't children who are forced to attend underfunded hazardous schools and deprived of educational opportunities precisely those whom Jesus called us to care for most?
4. Do you know why people in power continually deny African American children and their family's access to a good education by underfunding their schools?
5. Is it enough to try to equalize spending? Would that be enough to repair the harm done?

Response

1. Do you know if your elected representatives have been supporting legislation to require equitable funding of all schools? If not, why not?

- Could you find out?
- Could you write or call your elected representatives to tell them to do something about this injustice?

2. Do you know of any educational advocacy groups in your community?
3. Could you volunteer to help in any way to improve the education of African American children?
4. Would you be willing to seek out ways to volunteer to serve through mentoring, Big Sister, Big Brother, or college coaching?
5. Would you consider meeting with others to research ways of advocating for equal treatment of African American students?

Prayer Invitation

Abba, we beg you to gather into your heart all African American people and other people of color who suffer the injustice of being deprived of a good education. Embrace them and love them. Protect them from the politicians who have perpetuated this injustice. Grant them the grace of wisdom and understanding.

Abba, gather also into your heart all of those responsible for the injustice of racial segregation in education. By the power of your love, grant them wisdom, understanding, courage, and the will to recognize this injustice and to be inspired to bring about equal education for all children. Open the eyes and hearts of all people, especially those who vote, so that they see and respond to bring justice so that all children have access to a good education.

5

HEALTHCARE DISPARITIES

Of all the forms of inequality, injustice in health is one of
the most shocking and inhumane.

—Martin Luther King Jr.

TREATMENT DISPARITIES

During team rounds, the resident referred to a Black
patient by her first name, removed her bed clothes,
and examined her abdomen and breast without
drawing the curtain in a two-bed room. The next
patient (a white woman) who was called Mrs. Jones,
underwent the same examination while she was
carefully draped, and the curtain around her bed
was drawn.[1]

In the United States, if you have good health insurance, you have
access to the best healthcare in the world. But not all people in
the United States have access to healthcare. In 2017, more than
27 million Americans lacked health insurance.[2] In 2018, 11.5 percent of nonelderly Black Americans were uninsured, while 7.5
percent of white Americans lacked insurance. So in the United
States, millions of poor white, African American, and Hispanic
people have little or no access to healthcare.

Healthcare Disparities

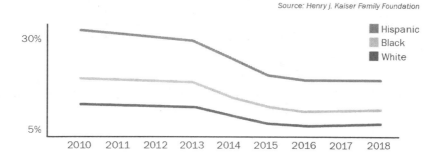

Source: Henry J. Kaiser Family Foundation

Figure 5: Uninsured Rates for Nonelderly Population by Race[3]

Even though the United States is the wealthiest country in the world, according to the Institute of Medicine of the National Academies it is the worst among advanced countries in several health outcomes including the following:[4]

- infant mortality and low birth weight
- obesity and diabetes
- heart disease
- chronic lung disease
- disability

People of color are treated *so poorly* by our healthcare system that their health outcomes drag the United States, with the best medical personnel and facilities in the world, to rank *last* among developed nations. Our healthcare system functions in ways diametrically opposed to the values of Jesus as expressed in his parable of the Good Samaritan.

The Heckler Report

The first study to report statistical differences in health and mortality because of unfair treatment of African American people in our healthcare system was the Heckler Report. In 1985, the U.S. Department of Health and Human Services reported an estimated eighteen thousand "excess deaths" each year among Black people because of heart disease and stroke. It also cited

8,100 deaths from cancer; 6,200 from infant mortality; and 1,850 from diabetes. Margaret Heckler, the Secretary of the Task Force, called this shameful inequity "an affront to both our ideals and to the ongoing genius of American medicine."[5]

Similar disparities were reported in 2003 in the study "Unequal Treatment: Confronting Racial and Ethnic Disparities in Healthcare," published by the National Research Council.[6] It drew on decades of research and found the following:

- The African American infant mortality rate was almost two and a half times that of white babies.[7]
- African Americans were more likely to be castrated as a treatment for prostate cancer.[8]
- African Americans received less pain medication for the same injuries and disease.[9]
- Surgeons did not operate on African American people as often for equally operable lung cancer.[10]
- Diabetic African Americans were more often amputated than diabetic whites. Nondiabetic Blacks were amputated more often too.[11]
- Compared with whites, African Americans had lower rates of cardiac surgeries, fewer hip and knee replacements, fewer kidney and liver transplants.[12]

In 2016, the National Institutes of Health reported the following in *Health Disparities*:

Overall, some disparities were getting smaller from 2000 through 2014–'15, but disparities persist, especially for poor persons and uninsured populations in all priority areas. While 20 percent of measures show disparities getting smaller for Blacks and Hispanics, *most disparities have not significantly changed for any racial or ethnic groups*.[13]

Disproportionate Deaths of African American People

The *New York Times* reported that in 2018, African American people died at higher rates than white people in nine of the top fifteen causes of death: heart disease (40 percent), diabetes (20 percent), cancer (19 percent), homicide (18 percent), stroke (16 percent), kidney (16 percent), hypertension (15 percent), septicemia (10 percent), and flu and pneumonia (2 percent). It also reported that if African American people had died at the same rate as white people in 2018, they would have avoided sixty-five thousand premature, excess deaths. Since 1900, the gap has caused 8.8 million Black people to die prematurely.[14]

This unjust treatment of African American people has been going on for four hundred years. It results in unnecessary suffering and death. It causes harm as surely as bullets from guns. It has been created by "respectable" people from afar—through law and policy. The perpetrators don't get to see the harm that they have caused. It is easy for anyone who lives in isolation of people of color to be unaware of this injustice because they cannot imagine the suffering it causes.

Disproportionate Deaths of African American Infants

What we politely call "health disparity" is killing people daily.

—Dayna Owen Matthew[15]

The death of a child is perhaps the worst thing that a parent can suffer. It affects everyone in the family: mother and father, siblings, grandparents, aunts and uncles. In 2016, the infant mortality rate for white infants was 4.9 deaths per 1,000 births. For African American infants, it was 11.3 deaths per 1,000 births. More than **two times** as many African American infants died as white infants.

Research has also shown that college-educated African American women were almost **three times** more likely to lose their infant than their similarly educated non-Hispanic white peers.[16] The reason African American babies are dying unnecessarily is not because of poverty. It is because of racism. Can you imagine how you would feel if your child or grandchild died because of lack of or inadequate treatment?

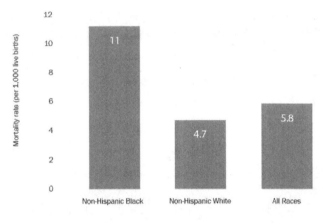

Source: "Infant Mortality and African Americans." U.S. Department of Health and Human Services. Office of Minority Health. https://minorityhealth.hhs.gov/omh/browse.aspx?lvl=4&lvlid=23

Figure 6: Infant Mortality Rate by Race[17]

MATERNAL MORTALITY RATES

In 2018, the Centers for Disease Control (CDC) reported that African American mothers die at **three to four times** the rate of non-Hispanic white mothers (see figure 7).[18] Research shows that Black women also experience more maternal health complications than white women.

- Black women are **three times** more likely to have fibroids (benign tumors that grow in the uterus and can cause postpartum hemorrhaging) than white women, and fibroids occur at younger ages and grow more quickly for Black women.[19]
- Black women experience physical "weathering," meaning their bodies age faster than white women's due to exposure to chronic stress, linked

to socioeconomic disadvantage and discrimination over the life course, making pregnancy riskier at an earlier age.[20]

- Black women experience more life-threatening complications during delivery.

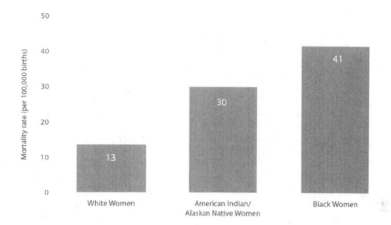

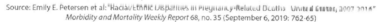

Source: Emily E. Petersen et al: "Racial/Ethnic Disparities in Pregnancy-Related Deaths United States, 2007-2016" *Morbidity and Mortality Weekly Report* 68, no. 35 (September 6, 2019: 762-65)

Figure 7: Maternal Mortality Rate by Race[21]

Severe Maternal Morbidity

Severe maternal morbidity (SMM) refers to life-threatening complications during delivery. The leading indicators of SMM include blood transfusion, disseminated intravascular coagulation, hysterectomy, ventilation, and adult respiratory distress syndrome. Women with underlying chronic conditions such as hypertension, diabetes, or heart disease were three times as likely to have SMM as women with no chronic conditions.

The New York City Department of Health and Mental Hygiene Bureau of Maternal, Infant, and Reproductive Health reported that Black non-Latino women are **three times** as likely to die during pregnancy or childbirth and **twice** as likely as white non-Latino women to experience severe maternal morbidity.[22]

A report in 2015 related to New York City pregnancy-associated mortality also found that Black non-Latino women were **twelve times** as likely as white non-Latino women to die from pregnancy-related causes.[23] It found there are likely many contributors to these disparities, including preconception health status, prevalence of obesity and other comorbidities, and access to care. Factors associated with poverty, such as inadequate housing, residential segregation, and lower education attainment, which disproportionately impact Black women, also increase the risk of SMM, and racism and its attendant stresses likely contribute to adverse maternal health outcomes as well.[24]

LIFE EXPECTANCY FOR AFRICAN AMERICAN PEOPLE

Rita Giordano reported in the *Philadelphia Inquirer* on a study that shows that there is a relationship between where you live and your health. Your zip code is a predictor of life expectancy. Giordano reports that if you lived in a white, middle- to upper-middle-class zip code just ten minutes from an African American inner-city zip code, your life expectancy was almost three decades longer.[25] It shouldn't come as a surprise that poverty affects health.

In consensus track 2055.03 in Lower Merion Township, the median income is $103,000. The township is 74 percent white. Just five miles away in consensus track 151.02 in North Philadelphia, the median income is approximately $14,000. Nearly 90 percent of the people are African American. The life expectancy in Philadelphia is sixty-four, versus ninety-two years in Lower Merion Township—a *twenty-eight-year* difference.

Giordano quoted Mariana Chilton, a professor at Drexel University's Dornsife School of Public Health:

> Lower-income Americans—and many are people of color—can find themselves virtually imprisoned in substandard housing and communities with failing schools,

in surroundings rife with governmental neglect....
It creates an enormous amount of stress and fear that
gets into your nervous system, which then affects your
organs and affects your brain—your cognitive, social,
and emotional development.[26]

It also affects how long you are likely to live.

OTHER HEALTH OUTCOME DISPARITIES

Donald A. Barr, MD, PhD, author of *Health Disparities in the United States*, did extensive research on the patterns and possible causes of racial disparities in access to care across a range of illnesses. He reported,

> I have looked at the treatment of ischemic heart disease, cancer, severe pain associated with traumatic injuries, treatment of kidney failure, and treatment of mental illness. I have found consistent patterns of care, with Blacks and Hispanics having less frequent access than whites to optimal medical treatment. I could have looked at other conditions and found the same pattern, such as access to replacement knee joints for seniors with severe arthritis (Skinner et al., 2003; Cisternas et al., 2009), access to flu shots for seniors (Schneider et al., 2001), or access to HPV vaccine for adolescents (Ylitalo and colleagues, 2013)....In each of the conditions I have looked at, I have found even greater disparities that seem to originate in the decisions physicians make about which treatments to apply in which patients.[27]

The following is a brief review of some research findings regarding healthcare disparities suffered by African American people.

Heart Disease

- African American adults are 40 percent more likely to have high blood pressure than their non-Hispanic white counterparts.[28]
- African American men are 50 percent more likely to have a stroke as compared to their white adult counterparts.[29]
- Black men are 60 percent more likely to die from a stroke as compared to non-Hispanic whites.[30]
- The incidence of sudden cardiac arrest among African American men was 175 per 100,000 people, compared to 84 per 100,000 for Caucasian men.[31]
- For African American women, the incidence of sudden cardiac arrest was 99 per 100,000, compared to 40 per 100,000 for Caucasian women.[32]

Asthma

- Black children have a 500 percent higher death rate from asthma compared to white children.[33]
- In 2015, African American women were found to be 20 percent more likely to have asthma than non-Hispanic whites.[34]
- In 2014, African Americans were almost **three times** more likely to die from asthma-related causes than the white population.[35]
- In 2015, African American children had a death rate **ten times** that of non-Hispanic white children.[36]
- Black children are **four times** more likely to be admitted to the hospital for asthma as compared to non-Hispanic white children.[37]

Cancer

- The American Cancer Society indicated that for most cancers, African Americans have the highest death rate and the shortest survival.[38]

- Black patients were the least likely to receive chemotherapy for colorectal cancer.[39]
- Black patients in the United States experience lower rates of survival after surgery for colorectal cancer.[40]
- From 2012 to 2016, African American women were just as likely to have been diagnosed with breast cancer, however, they were almost 40 percent more likely to die from breast cancer as compared to non-Hispanic white women.[41]
- From 2012 to 2016, African American men were 1.2 times and 1.7 times, respectively, more likely to have new cases of colorectal and prostate cancer.[42]
- African Americans can suffer from kidney failure at as much as **three times** the rate of Caucasians, according to the National Kidney Foundation.[43]

COVID-19'S EFFECT ON PEOPLE OF COLOR

Since the coronavirus, the unnecessary deaths of so many African American people by police, and the many protests of Black Lives Matter groups throughout the United States and the world, there has been an awakening to the insidiousness of the institutionalized violence of racism. Unfortunately, it took a pandemic, killings, and a protest to get the country to recognize the health disparities suffered by African American people. It did not take long for injury data to reveal the disproportionate sickness and death suffered by people of color as a result of COVID-19.

The CDC reported on November 30, 2020, that African American non-Hispanic people compared to white non-Hispanic people suffered[44]

- 2.6 times more coronavirus infections;
- 4.7 more hospitalizations; and
- 2.1 more deaths.

Risk factors that increase the likelihood of African American and Hispanic people dying include the following:[45]

- less access to healthcare
- greater prevalence of hypertension, obesity, diabetes, and lung disease
- living in neighborhoods lacking in healthy food options, green spaces, and recreational facilities
- greater use of public transportation
- living in densely populated areas
- more likely to be "essential workers"—bus drivers, food service workers, janitors, cashiers
- likely to work several jobs in caretaking (Black women in particular)
- more likely to be exposed to environmental hazards where they live

The CDC also reported on discriminatory risk factors that increased the risk of African American people getting sick and dying from COVID-19. Broadly, risks result from discrimination in healthcare, housing, education, occupation, criminal justice, and finance, including the following:[46]

- healthcare access and utilization
- over-representation in essential work settings such as healthcare, farms, factories, grocery stores, and public transportation; not being able to work from home; not having paid sick days
- education, income, and wealth gaps; having limited job options and less flexibility to leave jobs; unable to miss work, even if sick
- crowded living conditions likely for people from racial and ethnic minority groups

The coronavirus lifted the veil so no one could deny the existence of an intricate web of injustice that leads to African American people being disproportionately sickened and dying from COVID-19. What is now coming to light is how the coronavirus disproportionately harms children of color.

Healthcare Disparities

Roni Caryn Rabin reported in the *New York Times* that recent studies have renewed concerns about the susceptibility of children being infected by the coronavirus. She reported that children of color are affected at higher rates than white children and hospitalized at rates **five to eight times** that of white children. Children of color make up the overwhelming majority of those who develop a life-threatening complication called Multi-System Inflammatory Syndrome or MIS-C. So far (September 1, 2020), fewer than one hundred children have died of COVID-19. The majority were, however, children of color: forty-one Hispanic and twenty-four Black children. Of one thousand children tested in the State of Washington in March and April 2020, nearly half of the Hispanic children and nearly one-third of the Black children tested positive for the coronavirus.

Rabin pointed out two reports by the CDC in August that found Hispanic children were hospitalized at rates nearly **eight times** that of white children and Black children were hospitalized at rates **five times** that of white children. Another CDC paper looked at 570 children with MIS-C in forty states between March 2 and July 18, 2020. Of those whose race was known, only 13 percent were white; 40 percent were Hispanic, and 33 percent were Black.[47]

> When it is possible to point to where the system's ostensibly colorblind structure the race-based results are being produced, that structure has been racialized. When the policy produces racially disparate outcomes, but the cause is not formally built into the policy or the decision-making structure, the problem is systemic.[48]
>
> —Michigan Civil Rights Commission Report

Is it possible that our legislators, government officials, insurance company representatives, and hospital administrators are unconscious of this unfair treatment of people of color and poor white people? How many white people in positions of power participate silently in this injustice, draw their paychecks, and are seemingly unaware of what is happening? Are they oblivious to it all? If the tables were turned, would they remain silent?

APPLICATION

Catholic Social Teaching

Systematically, we must unmask social evil and, like prophets, denounce injustice. We must eradicate overt and covert racism. This requires solidarity with those suffering from disadvantages woven into society and our self-perceptions. For John Paul II, this solidarity is "not a feeling of vague compassion or shallow distress at the misfortunes of so many people....On the contrary, it is a firm and persevering determination to commit oneself to the common good."[49]

Reflection & Discussion

1. How did you feel when you read of the injustice in this chapter?
2. Can you imagine the heartbreak suffered by the mother, father, grandparents, and other loved ones after needlessly losing an infant in childbirth?
3. Can you imagine the heartbreak of a husband whose wife needlessly dies in childbirth?
4. Can you imagine the heartbreak caused by so many African American people dying needlessly because of a lack of healthcare or unfair treatment?
5. Do you know of anyone close to you who has no health insurance or who has been treated unfairly by a physician or the healthcare system?
6. How would you feel about a system and the powerful people who designed it if one of your loved ones was suffering a disease or injury and had no access to healthcare or was treated unfairly because of race or ethnicity?
7. How is it possible that legislators, insurance company officials, healthcare administrators, and others could create and perpetuate such a system?
8. If you were not aware of this injustice before, do you know why?

Response

1. Is it acceptable to you that millions of poor people lack access to healthcare?

   - Is there anything you can do politically to advocate for greater justice in healthcare access and treatment?
   - Is there anything you can do to awaken others to be aware of and do something about this injustice?

2. Are you beginning to understand how structural injustice harms precious people—mothers and fathers, infants and children, grandmothers and grandfathers—in so many ways?
3. Do you know of any groups who advocate for universal healthcare?
4. Do you know of any ways you could volunteer to assist advocacy groups advocating for universal healthcare?
5. Is there anything you could do to pressure your representatives to support universal healthcare?

Prayer Invitation

Abba, gather into your heart all of the people who have suffered or died needlessly because of their lack of healthcare. Gather the mothers and fathers who have lost children at birth because of a lack of or disparate medical treatment. Gather all of the husbands who have lost wives to disparate treatment during childbirth. Bless them, *Abba*, and comfort them. Bring new life from their suffering by awakening those who control this unfair system to see the magnitude and severity of the harm they are causing by this injustice. Open their hearts and minds so that they realize, before it is too late, that the system causing this injustice can easily be reversed. Grant them the courage and will to begin to end this injustice.

6

ENVIRONMENTAL RACISM

Many minority children are exposed to health hazards in their schools, only to come home to further exposures to environmental hazards from toxic waste sites and lead paint. Research shows a disproportionate amount of African American and Hispanic people are exposed to environmental hazards in their neighborhoods and in their houses. The research findings in this chapter come in large part from two studies: "Toxic Wastes and Race in the United States," completed in 1986, and "Toxic Wastes and Race at Twenty: 1987–2007," both produced by the Commission for Racial Justice of the United Church of Christ. Both studied uncontrolled toxic waste sites and commercial hazardous waste facilities, which potentially expose people nearby to lead, asbestos, arsenic, dioxin, TCE, DDT, PCBs, and other toxins.

"TOXIC WASTES AND RACE," 1986

The following gives a brief overview of the findings:[1]

Communities with Uncontrolled Hazardous Waste Sites

- Three out of every five African American people and Hispanic people lived in communities with uncontrolled toxic waste sites.

- More than 15 million African American people lived in communities with one or more uncontrolled toxic waste site.
- More than 8 million Hispanic people lived in communities with one or more uncontrolled toxic waste site.
- African American people were heavily overrepresented in populations in metropolitan areas with the largest number of uncontrolled toxic waste sites.

Commercial Hazardous Waste Facilities[2]

- Race proved to be the most significant among variables tested in association with the location of commercial hazardous waste site facilities. This represented a consistent national pattern.
- Communities with the greatest number of commercial hazardous waste sites had the highest composition of racial minorities.
- Although socioeconomic status appeared to play an important role in the location of commercial hazardous waste facilities, race still proved to be more significant.

"Toxic Wastes and Race: 1987–2007"

This report indicated that the conclusions found in 1986 were *very much the same* twenty years later with regard to where people and hazardous waste sites are located.

Key Findings

- Racial disparities in the distribution of hazardous waste sites were found to be greater than had been previously reported.[3]
- More than 9 million people (9,220,000) are estimated to live in circular host neighborhoods within three kilometers of the nation's 413

commercial hazardous waste facilities. More than 5.1 million people of color live in neighborhoods with one or more commercial hazardous waste facility.[4]

- Host neighborhoods of commercial hazardous waste facilities are 56 percent people of color.[5]
- Fully 105 of the 149 metropolitan areas with facilities (70 percent) have host neighborhoods with disproportionately high percentages of people of color, and forty-six of these metro areas (31 percent) have majority people of color in host neighborhoods.[6]
- Lead poisoning continues to be the number one environmental health threat to children in the United States, especially poor children, children of color, and children living in inner cities.[7]
- Black children are **five times** more likely than white children to have lead poisoning.[8]
- One in seven Black children living in older housing has elevated blood lead levels.[9]
- About 22 percent of African American children and 13 percent of Mexican American children living in houses built before 1946 are lead poisoned, compared with 6 percent of white children living in comparable types of housing.[10]
- Recent studies suggest that a young person's lead burden is linked to lower IQ, lower high school graduation rates, and increased delinquency.[11]

People of color now comprise the majority in neighborhoods with commercial hazardous waste facilities and make up more than two-thirds of the population in neighborhoods with clustered facilities. These reports also found that government officials have knowingly allowed families of people of color to live near superfund sites (U.S. locations that require a long-term response to properly clean up the contamination), other contaminated waste sites, and polluting industrial facilities poisoned with lead, arsenic, dioxin, TCE, DDT, PCBs, and a host of other deadly chemicals. According to the Environmental Protection

Agency, having the facts and failing to respond is explicitly discriminatory and tantamount to an immoral "human experiment."[12]

These two studies by the United Church of Christ reveal that people in power have shown a conscious disregard for the lives of minority people for decades. They have consciously permitted African American people and other people of color to be exposed to deadly toxins. In 2008, it found that essentially nothing had changed since 1987.

Environmental hazards increase the risk of cancer, lead poisoning, asbestosis, lung damage, and other diseases. All people exposed to these hazards are at risk but especially children and people who are elderly, sick, or already suffering a chronic illness. The sickness suffered by a family member also affects his or her parents, grandparents, and siblings. This tremendous toll is not being abated. A recent example of environmental racism is the contamination of drinking water in Flint, Michigan.

FLINT, MICHIGAN

In 2014, Flint, Michigan, switched its drinking water supply from Detroit's system to the Flint River to save money. Shortly thereafter, residents began to complain about foul-smelling, discolored, and off-tasting water. They complained for eighteen months because the water caused skin rashes, hair loss, and itching skin. At the time, they had not realized that they were also being exposed to lead poisoning, because Flint city officials maintained the water was safe. As we now know, however, the water was not safe. The Michigan Civil Rights Commission concluded that Flint's poor response to citizens' complaints was a "result of systemic racism."[13]

Studies revealed contaminated water contributed to doubling and, in some cases, tripling the incidents of elevated blood lead levels in the city's children. Even low lead levels can impair the brain development of fetuses, infants, and young children. The damage can reverberate for a lifetime, reducing IQ and physical growth, and contributing to anemia, hearing impairment, cardiovascular disease, and behavioral problems. Large doses of lead exposure in adults have been linked to high blood pressure, heart and kidney disease, and reduced fertility.

A study conducted in 2015 by researchers at Virginia Tech revealed the problem: Water samples collected from 250 homes indicated spiked citywide lead levels, with nearly 17 percent of the samples registering above the federal "action level" of 15 parts per billion (ppb), the level at which corrective action must be taken. More than 40 percent measured above 5 ppb of lead, which researchers considered an indication of a "very serious" problem. More alarming were the findings of Mona Hanna-Attisha, a Flint pediatrician, who found that blood lead levels across the city had nearly doubled since 2014. Nearly *nine thousand children were supplied lead-contaminated water* for eighteen months.

Flint's water supply was plagued by more than lead. The city's switch from Detroit's water to the Flint River coincided with an outbreak of Legionnaire's Disease (a severe form of pneumonia) that killed twelve and sickened at least eighty-seven people between June 2014 and October 2015.

In early 2016, Michigan Attorney General Bill Schuette announced a review to "determine what, if any, Michigan laws were violated" during Flint's drinking water disaster. On January 15, 2021, the *Philadelphia Inquirer* reported that nine people were charged for crimes related to a plan that contaminated the community with lead and contributed to nine Legionnaire's Disease deaths—the worst human-produced environmental disaster in history. Michigan Governor Rick Snyder was charged. His former health director, Nick Lyon, and ex-state medical executive, Eden Wells, were charged with involuntary manslaughter. Darnell Earley, the emergency manager in 2014, carried out a money-saving decision to use the Flint River for water while a pipeline from Lake Huron was under construction. The corrosive water was not treated properly, a misstep that freed lead from old plumbing into homes. Despite desperate pleas from residents holding jugs of discolored skunky water, the Snyder administration took no action until a doctor publicly reported elevated lead levels in children.

Richard Baird was charged with distortion, perjury, and obstruction of justice. Jarrod Agen, Governor Snyder's chief of staff, was charged with perjury. Howard Croft, former Flint Public Works director, was charged with willful neglect of duty. Nancy Peeler of the Health Department was charged with misconduct for allegedly concealing blood lead level analyses of children.[14]

CAMDEN COUNTY, NEW JERSEY

When I (Vince) lived in a suburb of Camden County in New Jersey, we had a wastewater treatment plant just a block and a half from our house. Occasionally it would back up. When it did, we could smell human waste. So real estate values in our part of town were lower. There were other sewage treatment plants in the white suburbs of Camden County. So politicians decided to build a new wastewater treatment plant to replace those in white neighborhoods and put it in the most highly populated area in the county, the City of Camden, where residents were overwhelmingly African American and Hispanic.

Real estate values near the wastewater treatment plant in Camden lowered because of the frequent releases of odors of human waste. Real estate values in my neighborhood went up. Can you imagine having a cookout with friends and family when a release occurs? Everyone would leave or go indoors. It could take hours to correct the problem. That is what used to happen to me and my white neighbors.

The mostly white people who controlled Camden County sent the problem to the City of Camden, one of the poorest cities in the United States, where African American and Hispanic people make up 94 percent of the population.

Sacred Heart Grammar School was located near the wastewater treatment plant in Camden. So was the Port Authority, where big, unprotected piles of sludge from a nearby refinery were stored. At the end of the school day, children could write their names in the dust from the sludge that was blown through the neighborhood and settled on their desks. The residents of South Camden organized and, after several years of advocacy, caused the Municipal Utility Authority to prevent backups from the wastewater treatment plant. Residents also caused the Port Authority to control the release of toxic dust to which the children and others were exposed. But it took years of struggle.

There have been many books, much research, and much reporting that sheds light on the fact that people of color without political and economic power have been exposed to many other environmental toxins much more frequently than middle- and upper-middle-income white people. That is, mostly white people in positions of power decide to protect their own and risk the lives of others. How many cancers were created? How many children suffered and are suffering from lead poisoning? How many elderly people died before their time? How many people already suffering from chronic diseases were further sickened? How many people are exposed to environmental hazards? How long will we continue to allow people of color to be needlessly exposed to the risk of cancer, lung disease, and brain damage?

Residential racism leads to environmental racism, which causes lower property values and adversely affects the health of people of color, as well as their wealth. Lead poisoning in children affects their mental capacity and ability to succeed in school and the likelihood of getting a good job. Moving waste treatment facilities from white communities to African American communities increases white people's home values and lowers African American people's home values. This web is intricately woven.

APPLICATION

Catholic Social Teaching

Bryan Massingale writes in *Racial Justice and the Catholic Church*,

> Racism has never been solely or principally about insults, slurs, or mere exclusion—racism entails more than conscious ill will, more than deliberate acts of avoidance, malice, and violence perpetuated by individuals....It is a set of cultural assumptions, beliefs, and convictions that justify the existence of a "kinder,

gentler" racism, that is, one that advocates interpersonal decency, kindness, and respect for all while it yet protects white systematic advantage and benefit.[15]

Reflection & Discussion

1. Imagine Jesus visiting the home of an African American family living in a neighborhood exposed to industrial toxins and meeting the parents of a child suffering from lead exposure. Can you imagine how he would feel?
2. Can you imagine how you would feel if your own child had high lead levels in her blood?
3. How would you feel if the local government officials decided to put a toxic waste site or wastewater treatment plant in your neighborhood?
4. How do you think you would feel about government officials who know that the people in your neighborhood are exposed to environmental toxins and do nothing about it?
5. How would you feel living in an environment that was making you physically ill and not having the resources to leave?

Response

1. Do you know if there are any toxic waste sites in the communities surrounding your community?

   - If not, have you ever investigated to see if there are?
   - If so, is there any environmental group or politician trying to cause remediation of the exposures?
   - Could you be of help?

2. Would you be interested in forming a small group to learn how to identify lead in paint and to volunteer to identify residences in need of remediation?

- Would you be willing to advocate for local authorities to respond?
- Is there anyone doing anything about lead in the paint in the houses in impoverished areas near your community?
- Could you be of help?

3. Do you know the position of any elected officials regarding environmental hazards in your city or state?
4. Do you have any desire to be involved in efforts to cause remediation of any environmental hazards suffered by people nearby?

Prayer Invitation

Abba, through your love of all people, those who suffer from environmental insults and those who create or tolerate them, protect the innocent and transform the hearts of those responsible. Grant them the courage, wisdom, and desire to protect your people from environmental hazards. Through your love, open the hearts of reporters to bring attention to this injustice so that politicians recognize the personal professional risk of perpetuating this injustice. Protect the health of those at risk, especially children, pregnant women, the sick, and the elderly.

7

VOTER SUPPRESSION

I swear to the Lord
I still can't see
Why democracy means
Everybody but me.

—Langston Hughes, *The Black Man Speaks*

The right to vote is the cornerstone of a democracy. Despite the fact that the right to vote is protected by the Fourteenth and Fifteenth Amendments, for more than 150 years, there have been efforts to prevent and suppress African American voters. This suppression continues today. Carol Anderson reports in her highly acclaimed book *One Person, No Vote* on the brutal race-based voter suppression of African Americans that has been destroying our democracy since the end of Reconstruction.

In 1867, during Reconstruction, Congress imposed military rule over most of the South to prevent the reestablishment of white supremacy. Because of that protection in the 1870s, one-half million Black men became voters. African Americans experienced significant changes in freedom of speech, the ability to travel, the right to a fair trial, and access to education. In the South, six hundred African Americans were elected to state government, fourteen to the U.S. Congress, two to the U.S. Senate, and many to other lower offices.[1]

This all changed in 1876 when the Supreme Court ruled that the Fifteenth Amendment protected only federal elections and that the states could impose their own voting restrictions. Things also changed in 1877 when Reconstruction ended, and federal troops were withdrawn from the South. Threats from employers and the Ku Klux Klan prevented African Americans from voting. Jim Crow laws began to be passed all over the South, including laws to make sure Blacks would never again participate in elections.

In 1890 in Mississippi, for example, white leaders held a convention to rewrite the Constitution. They made their intentions clear: "We came here to exclude the negro," declared the convention president.[2] The new state constitution required an annual poll tax that had to be paid two years before the election. It was a significant economic burden on Black Mississippians who were mostly poor. White leaders also passed literacy tests, understanding clauses, and good character clauses. Sixty percent of voting-age Black men, mostly former slaves, were prevented from voting because they were illiterate. Essentially all Black men were excluded, however, because when enforcing the "understanding" clause, the clerk would select complicated technical passages of the state constitution for them to interpret to prove their "understanding" of the constitution. The clerk would pass whites by picking simple sentences in the state constitution for them to explain. Mississippi cut the percentage of voting-age African American men registered to vote from more than 70 percent during Reconstruction to less than 6 percent in 1892.[3]

Anderson reports that Carter Glass, a Virginia representative, decided to bring the Mississippi Plan to Virginia. He planned not to "deprive a single white man of the ballot, but [to] inevitably cut from the existing electorate four-fifths of the Negro voters" in Virginia. When asked, "Will it be done by fraud and discrimination?" he answered, "By fraud, no. By discrimination, yes. Discrimination! Why this is precisely what we propose… to discriminate to the very extremity…permissible…under… the federal constitution, with a view to the elimination of every Negro voter who can be gotten rid of, legally, without materially impairing the numerical strength of the white electorate."[4]

These measures were copied by most of the other states in the South. These and other methods unfortunately proved successful until the passage of the Voter Rights Act in 1965. For example:[5]

- In Louisiana, where more than 130,000 Blacks had been registered to vote in 1896, the figure dropped to 1,342 by 1904.[6]
- African American registered voters in Alabama plunged from 180,000 to fewer than 3,000 in just three years.[7]
- In 1940, 3 percent of voting-age Black men and women in the South were registered to vote.[8]
- By 1953, in the Deep South, "eleven counties where the Black population equaled or exceeded that of whites" had only 1.3 percent of all eligible Blacks registered to vote. Two counties had no African American voters at all.[9]
- In 1867, the percentage of African American adults registered to vote in Mississippi was 66.9 percent. By 1955, it was 4.3.[10]
- Between 1954 and 1962, only eight Blacks in all of Clairborne County had managed to come through Mississippi's gauntlet.[11]
- In Mississippi, less than 1 percent were registered.
- Five counties in Alabama had zero to less than 2 percent of African Americans registered.[12]
- In 1962 in Georgia, less than 10 percent of age-eligible African Americans were registered in thirty counties with significant African American populations. In fact, four entire counties had fewer than ten nonwhites registered.[13]

THE VOTER RIGHTS ACT

On March 7, 1965, a day that came to be known as "Bloody Sunday," peaceful civil rights marchers crossed the Edmund Pettus Bridge in Selma, Alabama, on their way to the state capitol in Montgomery. The nation watched on television as state troopers and thugs attacked the marchers with barbed wire, bull whips, dogs, tear gas, and fire hoses, as police on horseback trampled them. As a result of that brutality, President Lyndon B. Johnson demanded the attorney general to craft a new law with teeth—the "goddamdest, toughest voting rights act that the attorney general could devise."[14]

The voting rights act passed and was signed into law on August 6, 1965. It put the federal government in the role of supervising voting in large parts of the country to protect African Americans' right to vote.

The impact of the VRA on African Americans was immediate. In Mississippi, Black registration went from less than 10 percent in 1964 to almost 60 percent in 1968; in Alabama, the figure rose from 24 percent to 57 percent. In the region as a whole, roughly one million new voters were registered within a few years after the bill became law, bringing African American registration to a record 62 percent.[15] However, those gains were essentially gutted by the Supreme Court in 2013 in *Shelby vs. Holder*.

The Brennan Center for Justice at the New York University School of Law reported that after the 2010 election, state lawmakers nationwide started introducing hundreds of laws and harsh measures making it harder to vote. The new laws ranged from strict photo ID requirements, to early voting cutbacks, to registration restrictions. Jelani Cobb, writing in *The New Yorker*, indicates that Chief Justice Roberts's vote *eviscerated* the Voter Rights Act of 1965.

The Civil Rights Act of 1964 required the federal government to scrutinize states that had a history of discrimination to prevent the passage of new election and voter laws that would discriminate against African American people. In his decision in *Shelby vs. Holder*, Chief Justice Roberts wrote that discrimination still exists but not sufficiently to warrant the "extraordinary" remediation measures that the act imposed on the states of the former Confederacy. He was, in effect, saying that things were okay now, so oversight is not necessary. Cobb argues that Roberts's decision is roughly the equivalent of saying that a decline in the prevalence of infectious disease means that we should stop vaccinating against it. Justice Ruth Bader Ginsberg pointed out that this decision was like throwing away your umbrella in a rainstorm because you are not getting wet.[16] Another analogy would be to decide to do away with enforcing highway speed limits because relatively few drivers are found to receive speeding tickets. Supreme Court justices are not naïve.

Roberts's decision is also similar to the decision of Judge Bohanon, who ruled in 1977 that because Oklahoma City had been declared in compliance with its school desegregation plan, it could be released from the order to desegregate. After the Bohanon decision, school districts around the country followed. Likewise, within hours of the *Shelby* decision, Texas announced a stricter new voter ID law. Mississippi and Alabama followed shortly thereafter, enforcing similar laws that had previously been barred.

Justification for Voter Suppression Tactics—Voter Fraud

The finest trick of the devil is to persuade you that he does not exist.

—Charles Baudelaire

The argument made for passing voter restriction laws is to prevent voter fraud. That justification is itself fraudulent. Research shows that there is no evidence of significant voter fraud.

The Brennan Center for Justice at New York University provides a compilation of dozens of voter fraud studies, analyses, government actions, and court rulings. Evidence suggests that voter fraud is *exceptionally rare*. It essentially found that claims of voter fraud by Republican politicians and pundits are not based on facts. They are based on lies. That is, political strategists deliberately created the notion of voter fraud to justify silencing the voice of the most vulnerable people. They sought to gain and maintain control over political decisions and to keep in place the structural injustice and institutional violence that harms the most vulnerable, that is, African American people and other people of color.

The Brennan Center reported the following:

- Elections meticulously studied for voter fraud found incident rates between 0.0003 percent and 0.0025 percent.[17]

- The *Washington Post* reported thirty-one credible instances of impersonation fraud from 2000 to 2014 out of more than one billion ballots cast over that time.[18]
- Election officials who surveyed forty-two jurisdictions and oversaw the tabulation of 23.5 million votes in the 2016 general election found that officials referred only an estimated thirty incidents of suspected noncitizen voting for further investigation or prosecution. That comes to a noncitizen voting rate of 0.0001 percent among those jurisdictions.[19]
- The Fifth Circuit in Texas in 2016 found "only two convictions" for in-person voter impersonation fraud out of twenty million votes cast in the decade before Texas passed its laws.
- In North Carolina in 2016, the Fourth Circuit noted that the state "failed to identify even a single individual who has ever been charged with committing in-person voter fraud in North Carolina."

VOTER RESTRICTIONS

Overall, twenty-five states have put in place new voter restrictions. Fifteen states have more restrictive voter ID laws in place (and six states have strict photo ID requirements), twelve have laws making it harder for citizens to register, seven cut back on early voting opportunities, and three made it harder to restore voting rights for people with past criminal convictions.[20]

In 2016, fourteen states had new voting restrictions in place for the first time in a presidential election. Those fourteen states were Alabama, Arizona, Indiana, Kansas, Mississippi, Nebraska, New Hampshire, Ohio, Rhode Island, South Carolina, Texas, Tennessee, Virginia, and Wisconsin. In 2017, legislators in Arkansas and North Dakota passed voter ID bills, which governors in each state signed, and Missouri implemented a restrictive law that was passed by ballot initiative in 2016. Georgia, Iowa, Indiana, and New Hampshire also enacted restrictions in 2018, in addition to laws that were on the books for previous elections.[21]

The American Civil Liberties Union in its Fact Sheet (2014) "Oppose Voter ID Legislation" published the following regarding voter ID legislation:

> Thirty-four states have identification requirements at the poll. Seven have strict ID laws....Voter ID laws deprive many voters of the right to vote, reduce participation, and stand in direct opposition to our country's trend of including more Americans in the democratic process. Many Americans do not have one of the forms of identification states acceptable for voting.

The Carter-Ford Commission estimated that approximately nineteen million potential voters did not have either a driver's license or a state-issued ID photo. It found that those "most likely to be adversely affected...were disproportionately young, elderly, poor, and African American."[22] This was key. All that had to happen was for the GOP to enforce the lie of voter fraud, create the public perception of democracy imperiled, increase the groundswell to "protect the integrity of the ballot box," require exactly the type of identification that Black, poor, young, and elderly persons did not have, and, equally important, mask these acts of aggressive voter suppression behind the nobility of being "civic minded." From 2005 to 2013, Republicans did just that.[23]

Powerful white people designed ways to restrict the most vulnerable in America from voting. They surely know that what they are doing is silencing the voice of people who have the "least" power. Senator Dick Durbin writes,

> Republican-led legislators continue to enact laws making it harder for a significant number of Americans to exercise their fundamental right to vote. Evidence suggests their plan is working. A recent study found that in the 2016 election, Wisconsin voter ID law deterred nearly 17,000—and perhaps as many as 23,000—eligible voters in two counties from casting

ballots. President Trump's margin of victory in Wisconsin was only 22,748 votes.[24]

Senator Durbin has said that the right to vote is even under greater assault today.

EX-OFFENDER DISENFRANCHISEMENT

The United States is one of the world's strictest nations when it comes to denying the right to vote to citizens convicted of crimes. Americans numbering 5.85 million are forbidden to vote because of "felon disenfranchisement," or laws restricting voting rights for those convicted of felony-level crimes.

The Sentencing Project has found the following facts:[25]

- The number of people disenfranchised due to a felony conviction has escalated dramatically in recent decades as the population under criminal justice supervision has increased. There were an estimated 1.17 million people disenfranchised in 1976, 3.34 million in 1996, and over 5.85 million in 2010.
- The rates of disenfranchisement vary dramatically by state due to broad variations in voting prohibitions. In six states—Alabama, Florida, Kentucky, Mississippi, Tennessee, and Virginia—more than 7 percent of the adult population is disenfranchised.
- One in every thirteen African Americans of voting age is disenfranchised, a rate more than four times greater than non-African Americans. Nearly 7.7 percent of the adult African American population is disenfranchised compared to 1.8 percent of the non-African American population.
- African American disenfranchisement rates also vary significantly by state. In three states—Florida (23 percent), Kentucky (22 percent), and Virginia

(20 percent)—more than one in five African
Americans is disenfranchised.

Ari Berman reported in *The Nation* that prior to the 2000
presidential election, Florida sent its county election supervisors
a list of fifty-eight thousand alleged felons to purge from voting
rolls. Blacks made up only 11 percent of registered voters in Florida, but 44 percent of those on the purged list. The purged list
turned out to be littered with errors. The Civil Rights Commission launched a major investigation into the 2000 election. Acting
general counsel, Edward Hailes, found that if twelve thousand
were wrongly purged from the rolls, and 44 percent of them were
African American, and 90 percent of African Americans voted
for Al Gore, that meant 4,752 Black Gore voters—almost nine
times George W. Bush's margin of a victory—could have been
prevented from voting. Berman reported, "It's not a stretch to
conclude that the purge cost Gore the election." "We did think it
was outcome-determinative," Hailes said.[26]

The claim of "voter fraud" as justification to suppress African American people's votes was never more severe and obvious than during and after the 2020 election. The *New York Times*
called President Trump's baseless and desperate claims of a stolen election the most aggressive promotion of "voter fraud" in
American history.[27] The *Times* reported that Trump's efforts led
to "a thorough debunking of the sorts of voter right claims that
Republicans have used to roll back voting rights for the better
part of a century."

Rather than present facts of voter fraud in their legal argu-
ments, Trump's lawyers used unfounded rumors similar to those
Republicans have used to justify laws that in many cases made
voting disproportionately harder for Blacks and Hispanics, who
largely support Democrats. The *Times* further reported,

Their allegations that thousands of people "double
voted" by assuming other identities at polling booths
echoed those that had previously been cited as reason
to impose stricter new voter identification laws.

Their assertion that legal numbers of non-citizens
cast illegal votes for Biden matched claims Republicans

105

have made to argue for harsher new "proof of citizenship" requirements for voter registration.

Their tales about larger numbers of cheaters casting ballots in the name of "dead voters" were akin to those several states have used to conduct aggressive "purges" of voting lists that wrongfully slated tens of thousands of registrations from termination.

After bringing some sixty lawsuits, and even offering financial incentive for information about fraud, Mr. Trump and his allies have failed to prove definitively any case of illegal voting on behalf of their opponents in court—not a single case of an undocumented immigrant casting a ballot, a citizen double voting, nor any credible evidence that legions of voting dead gave Mr. Biden a victory that was not his.

Kristen Clarke, President of the National Lawyers Committee for Civil Rights Under Law and former Justice Department attorney, commented on the failed efforts of Republicans to suppress votes: "It really should put a death knell in this narrative that has been peddling around claims of voter fraud that has never been substantiated. They put themselves on trial, and they failed."

On January 6, 2021, Trump continued telling his supporters the Big Lie that the election was stolen from him. He incited tens of thousands to storm the Capitol to disrupt the peaceful transition of power and prevent our democracy from functioning. We almost lost our democracy.

The Big Lie continues to put our democracy at risk. Only U.S. Representative Liz Cheney and Senator Mitt Romney among Republicans have had the courage to say the election was not stolen by fraud. Federal judges have found some of the claims of voter fraud to be so outrageous that they were denounced as unethical attempts to disenfranchise millions of voters.[28] Since the election, Republican legislators have introduced bills to further restrict voters in forty-seven states.[29] Our democracy is still at risk.

Historically, voter suppression tactics designed by powerful white politicians have been effective in barring African American people from sharing power. They are designed to keep the power in the hands of white people. These are not "misguided" politicians. They are people who misguide the electorate. They use diabolical tactics, that is, the lie of voter fraud, to maintain power and control of the lives of others.

APPLICATION

Catholic Social Teaching

"Open Wide Our Hearts: The Enduring Call to Love," a pastoral letter against racism from the U.S. Conference of Catholic Bishops, quotes Pope Francis:

> The roots of racism have extended deeply into the soil of our society. Racism can only end if we contend with the policies and institutional barriers that perpetuate and preserve the inequity—economic and social—that we still see all around us. With renewed vigor, we call on the members of the Body of Christ to join others in advocating and promoting policies at all levels that will combat racism and its effect in our civic and social institutions.... "Our efforts must aim at restoring hope, righting wrongs, maintaining commitments, and thus promoting the well-being of individuals and of peoples."[30]

Reflection & Discussion

1. Were you aware of the ways African American people's voices have been silenced for more than 150 years?
2. Imagine how Jesus, who was so critical of hypocrisy, would feel about the politicians and government officials in a democracy conspiring and lying to prevent the least influential and most oppressed people from voting.

   • How do you feel about this hypocrisy?

3. Before reading this chapter, did you think there was significant fraudulent voting in the United States?
4. How do you think African American people feel when they hear of or read of politicians creating tactics to suppress their vote?
5. Have you ever read of efforts by anyone or any group to try to prevent your vote?

Response

1. Do you know if there are unjust voter restrictions in your state?
2. Do you know your elected representatives' positions on laws that restrict African American voters?
3. Could you contact your representatives about voter suppression tactics?
4. Could you write a letter to the editor of a newspaper about this injustice?
5. Do you know of any advocacy groups working to prevent voter restriction?

   • Do they offer service opportunities for volunteers?

Prayer Invitation

Abba, awaken the hearts and minds of the perpetrators of the voter fraud myth so that they become aware of how they are harming those with the least amount of political influence. Help them to hear the words of Jesus: whatever you do to these, the least of my people, you do to me.

Abba, help them to see the hypocrisy of a Christian or any person of faith trying to suppress the voice of the oppressed. Grant wisdom and courage to all people trying to counter this injustice: reporters, teachers, clergy, politicians, and others.

8

WEALTH AND INCOME DISPARITIES

Woe to him who builds his house by unrighteousness,
    and his upper rooms by injustice;
who makes his neighbors work for nothing,
    and does not give them their wages.

—Jeremiah 22:13

The Institute for Policy Studies has found that the median African American family with just over $3,500 of wealth owns just 2 percent of the nearly $140,000 median white family wealth. The median white family has **forty-one times** more wealth than the median African American family![1]

It is not because God has endowed white people with greater intelligence, initiative, or a better work ethic that most white people earn more and have more wealth than most African American people. It took centuries of slavery, Jim Crow, and the systematic injustice and institutionalized violence of racism to create the huge gap in income and wealth that exists today between African American and white people. When we see how this injustice began and was perpetuated, we can see the tremendous benefits and advantages that middle- and upper-class white people have had and still have over African American people.

SLAVERY—THE FUEL FOR ECONOMIC GROWTH

> Planter: "You lazy n—, I'm losing a whole day's labor by you."
>
> Freed Man: "Massa, how many days labor have I lost by you?"
>
> —Eric Foner, *Forever Free*

Slavery has provided massive financial benefits to white people from increased profits that resulted from the abuse, torture, and suffering of African American people. "Control" of enslaved people was key to increasing productivity and economic growth. It was established through whippings, shackles, branding, mutilations, torture, and imprisonment. Southern white elites and northern textile mill owners grew rich. Their wealth was passed on to their descendants through inheritance. Slavery was used to fuel the Industrial Revolution. After slavery, African American people were controlled through Black Codes, mass incarceration, and convict leasing.

Black Codes and Convict Leasing: Slavery by Another Name

As indicated in chapter 1, many thousands of African American people convicted of minor Black Code violations were imprisoned and sent to work in factories, mills, farms, and mines to pay for the costs associated with their imprisonment. Their labor provided the equivalent of tens of millions of dollars to the treasuries of Alabama, Mississippi, Louisiana, Georgia, Florida, Texas, North Carolina, and South Carolina.[2] Their labor enriched the bank accounts of the white owners of the businesses where they worked. Their white descendants today are beneficiaries of the wealth handed down from generation to generation.

The practice of arrests, prosecution, and sale of convict labor to corporations is not a thing of the past. It continues today through Federal Prison Industries, Inc. In 1934, Franklin Delano Roosevelt signed an executive order creating Federal Prison Industries, Inc., known as UNICOR. It has provided work for

110

prisoners. Today, federal prisoners work in factories producing clothing, textiles, electronics, vehicle components, office furniture, farm produce, and so on. UNICOR advertises that it provides federal prisoners with opportunities to develop life skills that enhance their likelihood of finding employment upon release from prison. Former offenders are 24 percent less likely to recidivate than nonparticipating inmates. They are also paid wages lower than workers in the poorest countries in the world.[3]

Prisoners who refuse to provide labor can be put in solitary confinement. In *Mikeska vs. Collins*, decided in 1990, the court ruled that inmates who refused to be forced into indentured servitude by prison work assignments that provided no minimum wage could be thrown into solitary confinement. Ben Crump reports in *Open Season* that the court made it abundantly clear that inmates have no choice: they will work as slaves for the state, under whatever terms and conditions the prison chooses, and if they don't, they can and will be punished. While generating an estimated $2 billion in annual revenue for federal, state, and local governments and for private contractors, inmates receive an average wage for an entire day's work that equals less than the minimum wage for one hour of work.[4] Even today, the work of African American prisoners is "subsidizing" the profit of corporations in the United States by enriching corporations.

Sharecropping

After the Civil War, white landowners needed laborers. African American people could provide labor. So the system of sharecropping was established. The landowner assigned each African American family a small plot of land, or "share," of the farm and provided food, shelter, and clothing, as well as seeds and farm equipment. By contract, at harvest, the farmer took the cotton to market and, after deducting the costs of seeds, equipment, rent, and food, agreed to give one-half of the proceeds to the African American family. Under this system, African American workers continued to work in ways *quite similar to slavery*. The landowner restored gang labor and centralized plantations, and provided close "supervision" of the work and social lives of African American families. When landowners demanded higher percentages of profit, there was a risk of a response from share-croppers because of the obscenely low wages.

The sharecropping system became a way for white farm owners to get sharecroppers indebted and then swearing out warrants accusing them of fraud.[5] When facing a white judge, sharecroppers would typically "confess judgment." The local judge would then accept as payment a contract signed by the sharecropper to work without payment for however long it took to pay back the debt. This practice spread throughout the South in the 1880s and 1890s. The result was Black tenant farmers and sharecroppers often returning to the same fields where they had worked as freed persons, providing uncompensated labor, sub-jected to imprisonment, shackles, and the lash. White farmers often continued the indebtedness by adding time to work off the cost of doctor visits, medicine, clothing, damaged tools, or hous-ing costs. Sharecroppers were also subjected to violence if they tried to resist. Francine Uenuma reports on the massacre that occurred when sharecroppers in Elaine, Arkansas, organized to try to attain some measure of economic justice.[6]

Elaine Massacre of 1919

On the night of September 30, 1919, approximately one hundred African American sharecroppers attended a meeting of the Progressive Farmers and Household Union of America at a church three miles north of Elaine, Arkansas. They were upset because landowners were demanding higher and higher per-centages of profit without ever presenting an accounting. Land-owners were trapping them with "supposed debts." The leaders placed armed guards around the church to prevent a disruption of their meeting.

At around eleven o'clock that night, a group of local white men fired shots into the church. The shots were returned and, in the chaos, one white man was killed. Rumors arose that share-croppers were leading an organized "insurrection" against the white residents of Phillips County.

Governor Charles Brough called for five hundred soldiers to "round up" the "heavily armed Negros." The troops were "under order to shoot and kill any negro who refused to surrender immediately." They indiscriminately killed men, women, and children: at least two hundred deaths are documented, but estimates are much higher.

Convict labor and sharecropping were not the only way that African Americans have been "subsidizing" corporations owned by white people. The prices of products produced in our factories by other African American workers throughout our history were also subsidized by the lives of African American workers who were exposed to workplace hazards that resulted in catastrophic injury, disease, and death.

INJURY AND DISEASE SUFFERED BY AFRICAN AMERICAN WORKERS

It is very common for African Americans to be given the most dangerous jobs in our manufacturing industries.[7] Research shows that African American workers suffer disproportionate workplace injury and disease. For instance:

- African American workers have a 37 percent greater chance of suffering an occupationally induced injury or disease and a 20 percent greater chance of dying from an occupational disease or injury than do white workers. Black workers are almost twice as likely to be partially disabled because of job-related injury or disease.[8]
- There are an estimated 313,000 farm workers in the United States who suffer pesticide-related illness each year. Ninety percent of the approximately two million farm workers are people of color.[9] For a great many years, researchers have found that most farm pesticide exposures occur among low-income Latin American and African American immigrants.[10]
- The U.S. Public Health Department study of chromate workers found that the expected cancer mortality rate for African Americans was an alarming 80 percent; it was 14.27 percent for white people.[11]

- A study of fifty-nine thousand steel workers showed that 89 percent of nonwhite coke plant employees were assigned to work in the coke oven (one of the most hazardous aspects of steel production), while only 32 percent of white employees had worked in that area of the plant. Nonwhite employees in coke plants experienced double the expected cancer-related death rate.[12]
- The National Institute of Occupational Safety and Health (NIOSH) concluded that research shows that "minority workers tend to encounter a disproportionately greater number of serious safety hazards because they are employed in especially dirty and dangerous jobs.[13] NIOSH's conclusion is supported by data indicating that mortality from acutely hazardous work exposures among men of color is 50 percent higher than it is among white men.[14]

Exposing workers to hazards violates the Occupational Safety and Health Act of 1970, which requires employers to provide workers a work environment free of recognized hazards. There are significant costs, however, associated with eliminating and controlling occupational hazards. Employers who violate the law and permit workers to be exposed to workplace hazards can save the costs of hazard control. When they do, they shift the economic burden to workers who suffer this injustice by losing their jobs, suffering disability and disease, and sometimes losing their lives. Corporate owners have benefited financially from this injustice for centuries. This economic benefit to corporate owners has been paid for by the blood, sweat, tears, and sometimes even lives of African American people. Today, some white people feel that affirmative action policies meant to provide opportunities to minority people are unfair because they discriminate against white people. With an understanding of history, you will see that our government has been implementing laws and policies designed to benefit mostly white people for a long time. Affirmative action for white people is the bedrock of our economic system.

LAND REDISTRIBUTION— THE HOMESTEAD ACTS

Despite General Sherman's promise of forty acres and a mule, no land or mules were provided to freed people. Instead, Congress passed the Homestead Acts. Between 1868 and 1934, by way of the Homestead Acts, the federal government gave away 246 million acres in 160-acre tracts, that is, nearly 10 percent of the nation, to more than 1.5 million white families, native born and foreign. Forty million Americans today, nearly 20 percent of all American adults, descended from these homesteaders.[15] The Homestead Acts were the most extensive, radical, redistributive government policy in American history. They created untold wealth for white people and their descendants living today. Talk about discriminatory affirmative action!

In the forty-five years after the Civil War, African American people accumulated roughly 15 million acres, mostly in the South. By 1920, there were 925,000 Black-owned farms, representing about 14 percent of all of the farms in the United States. Land was then systematically taken from African American people through the violence of White Caps and the deviousness of partition sales. By 1997, African American people lost 90 percent of their farmland.[16]

WHITE CAPS

White Caps were societies of poor white farmers, frequently sharecroppers or small landowners, who operated to control African American people and prevent them from buying land. They were associated with the Ku Klux Klan. At the end of the nineteenth century, members of the White Caps beat and threatened African American farmers if they didn't abandon their homes and farms. For example, for more than two months in 1912, violent white mobs in Forsyth County, Georgia, drove out almost the entire Black population—more than a thousand people. Prosperous African American people were a threat to the notion of white supremacy. The Associated Press documented

57 other violent land grabs among 107 others involving trickery and legal manipulations.[17] One method of legal manipulation was partition sales.

PARTITION SALES

Partition sales refers to a tactic used by developers to gain control of land owned by African American people. Officially sanctioned by the courts, this process targeted the heirs of property of people who did not have clear title to the land, mainly African American people. Seventy-six percent of African American people do not have wills or estate plans, so at death, their land goes to their descendants. After time, the number of heirs that share ownership in the land increases significantly. For example, after a mother and father pass, their five children would each own one-fifth of the land. If each of those children has five children, there would then become twenty-five owners. As time goes on, there would be more and more owners of the property. Below is a description of how partition sales worked.

If one of the heirs decided to sell the land, it could be legally sold at auction despite objections by all of the other heirs. That is, one person with one share could petition the court to sell the entire property at auction against the will of the other heirs. So, if a developer could entice only one of the many owners to sell his or her share, the land would be sold.

Studies show that auctions result in a sale in value of only a tiny percent of the actual value of the land.[18] There was also the risk of the heirs who are living on the property being forced to sell because they could not keep up with repairs or pay taxes. They were more likely to be forced to sell because, without title, they were not eligible to apply for state and federal housing aid. They could not get a mortgage or do extensive repairs to their homes. They were not eligible to apply for state or federal housing aid, such as funds provided by the Federal Emergency Management Agency or for nearly any of the programs administered by the Department of Agriculture, including the crucial Loans and Conservation Funding that keep many rural landowners afloat.[19] So an African American family living on the land was at risk of being forced to sell for economic reasons or because one of the heirs was enticed to sell by a developer.

A 2001 report of the U.S. Department of Agricultural Consensus estimated that about *80 percent of Black-owned farmlands had disappeared* in the South since 1969.[20] By 1997, African Americans had lost *90 percent* of their farmland. A group of economists and statisticians recently calculated that, since 1910, African American families have been stripped of *hundreds of billions of dollars* because of lost land.[21]

FURTHER GOVERNMENT PARTICIPATION IN ECONOMIC DISPARITIES

The following are only a few of the ways that our government has designed programs to benefit white people's ability to earn income and accumulate wealth and to *restrict* African American people from doing the same.

The New Deal: 1933–1939

In 1933, the Roosevelt administration established the New Deal to help the country get back on its feet after the Great Depression. The New Deal was a set of public work projects, regulations, and financial reforms. The following are some of the New Deal programs that disproportionately benefitted white people.

Federal Emergency Relief Administration (FERA)

The FERA, adopted in 1933, was created to provide jobs. It disproportionately spent funds on unemployed whites and frequently refused to permit African Americans to take any but the least skilled jobs. It also paid African Americans less than the official stipulated wage.[22]

The Federal Housing Administration (FHA)

The FHA was established to help citizens buy homes. But it excluded African American people. As indicated in chapter 3, "Residential Segregation," the FHA created color-coded maps that drew red lines around African American neighborhoods and excluded them from federal homeownership assistance. Ninety-eight percent of the loans of the FHA insured from 1932 to 1962 went to white Americans, locking nearly all Black Americans out of the government program credited with building the modern (white) middle class.[23]

The National Recovery Administration (NRA)

The NRA established minimum wages and social security for workers in particular industries. However, it *excluded* many industries in which primarily African American workers were employed, such as the domestic service industry, the agricultural industry, and many subindustries such as canning, citrus packing, cotton ginning, and others.[24]

Civilian Conservation Corps (CCC)

The CCC was a relief program for unemployed, unmarried men that offered these young men employment in environmental projects. Some states did not permit African American men to enroll at all. But when they were permitted to enroll, they were restricted to menial jobs so they could not develop the higher skills that the corps was meant to provide. Florida announced it would not accept African Americans at all. Texas officials declared that "this work is for whites only."[25]

The government's participation in blocking African Americans' wage-earning opportunities had its most devastating effect during World War II, when Black workers migrated to centers of war production in search of jobs.

Fair Labor Standard Act of 1938

The Fair Labor Standard Act provided a minimum wage, overtime benefits of time and a half for hours worked more than forty per week, and child labor laws. It excluded farm workers and domestic workers, that is, those jobs most commonly held by African American people.

World War II

The Roosevelt administration required factories to convert from civilian to military production during the war. The military operated shipbuilding yards and ammunition, aircraft, and tank manufacturers. Yet, federal agencies tolerated and supported joint labor management policies that kept African Americans in the most poorly paid jobs in defense plants. For example, the San Francisco Bay area had the largest center of war-related shipbuilding in the nation. Membership in the Maritime Laborers Union and Steamfitters Union soared from four hundred to seventeen thousand. Unions like the Steamfitters Union had National Labor Relation Board certified agreements requiring companies to not hire without a union referral. *The unions would not refer African Americans.*[26] The government permitted the unions controlled by white men to prevent African American workers from getting good-paying jobs to support their families. It was just standard accepted practice.

The GI Bill

In 1944, the GI Bill was adopted to help returning servicemen buy homes. It created the middle class but almost exclusively for white people. It provided veterans the opportunity to get a mortgage without a down payment. It enabled nearly five million white people to buy homes.[27] In New York and northern New Jersey, fewer than one hundred of the sixty-seven thousand mortgages issues by the Veterans Administration supported homes purchased by nonwhites.[28] The Veterans Administration not only denied African Americans the mortgage subsidies to which they were entitled, but also frequently restricted African Americans to education and training benefits for only lower-level jobs and, in some cases, refused to process applications to four-year colleges for African Americans.[29]

CONTRACT BUYING

Contract buying of houses was another scheme designed to extract wealth from African American families. Normally, a homeowner takes out a mortgage loan and begins to make monthly payments of interest and principal. Each month, the amount owed to the bank goes down. And each month, the homeowner accumulates more equity or more ownership of the house. If they were to sell the house after ten years, they would pay off the loan to the bank and receive the equity or amount of money they paid to the bank in principle. They would also receive as profit the difference between the purchase price and the selling price, which historically goes up. However, because of redlining[30] and other discriminatory lending practices, African American people were unlikely to be approved for a standard bank mortgage. The scheme of contract buying was created. It significantly limited the possibility of African American families benefiting from the purchase of homes.

Contract buying worked like this: A buyer puts down a large down payment for a home and makes monthly installments at high interest rates. But the buyer never gains ownership until the contract is paid in full and all the conditions are met. Meanwhile, the contract seller holds the deed and could evict the buyer if even just one payment were missed. Contract buyers accumulated no equity in their homes. No laws or regulations protected them. Home contract sales were ruthlessly exploitive means of extracting capital from African Americans who had no better alternatives in their pursuit of homeownership. A report published by the Samuel DeBois Cook Center on Social Justice reported the following:[31]

- Between 75 percent and 95 percent of homes sold to Black families during the 1950s and 1960s were sold on contract.
- The markup price on homes sold on contract was 84 percent.
- African Americans who bought on contract paid, on average, an additional $587 (in current dollars) more a month than if they had a conventional mortgage.

During the 1950s and 1960s, Black families in Chicago lost between *$3 billion and $4 billion in wealth* because of predatory housing contracts. Contract buying was widespread, not only in Chicago, but also in Baltimore, Cincinnati, Detroit, Washington, D.C., and elsewhere.[32]

DISCRIMINATORY PROPERTY ASSESSMENTS

City governments assess properties to determine the tax rate for that property. Richard Rothstein shows that in the mid-twentieth century, city and county governments extracted excessive taxes from African Americans by overassessing properties in Black neighborhoods and underassessing them in white neighborhoods.[33] For example, in 1973, in a study of ten large U.S. cities, the Federal Department of Housing and Urban Development found a systematic pattern of overassessment in low-income African American neighborhoods, with corresponding underassessment in white middle-class neighborhoods.[34] That is, city governments required poor African American people to pay higher property taxes than white people in more affluent neighborhoods. For example:

- In Baltimore, the property tax burden in the white middle-class community of Gilford, near Johns Hopkins University, was one-ninth that of African American East Baltimore.[35]
- In Philadelphia, the tax burden in white middle-class South Philadelphia was one-sixth that of African American North Philadelphia.[36]
- In Chicago, the tax burden of white middle-class Norfolk was one-half that of African American Woodlawn.

Excessive taxation made it more likely that African American families would be delinquent in tax payments and more likely to be prey for speculators who could seize their homes without paying off the taxes and then resell the houses at an enormous profit.[37] Discriminatory assessments were the result of city assessors' violations of the U.S. Constitution. That is, city governments throughout the country systematically violated the Constitution by requiring poor African American homeowners to pay taxes at a much higher rate than white people.

REVERSE REDLINING

In December 2019, the City of Philadelphia settled a suit with Wells Fargo Bank for $10 million based on the bank's predatory mortgage loan practices that singled out minority homeowners for more expensive and riskier mortgage loans than their white counterparts—a practice known as reverse redlining. The *Philadelphia Inquirer* editorial reported that Wells Fargo is not the only bank nor is Philadelphia the only settlement of reverse redlining lawsuits. This pervasive long-term practice keeps minorities away from the primary source of wealth for most people: real estate. The efforts to restrict minorities have been successful, considering that 80 percent of those below the poverty level in Philadelphia are not white.[38]

DEVALUATION OF HOMES IN AFRICAN AMERICAN NEIGHBORHOODS

A study by the Brookings Institute found that houses in neighborhoods of 50 percent or more African American people are valued at roughly one-half the price as homes in neighborhoods with no African American residents. It found that homes of similar quality in neighborhoods with similar amenities are worth 23 percent less in majority Black neighborhoods, compared to those with very few or no Black residents. Majority Black neighborhoods do exhibit features associated with lower property values, including higher crime rates, longer commute times, and less access to high-scoring schools and well-rated restaurants. Yet, these factors only explain roughly half of the under-evaluation of homes in Black neighborhoods. Across all majority Black neighborhoods, owner-occupied homes are undervalued by *$48,000 per home* on average, amounting to *$156 billion* in cumulative losses.[39]

One significant reason for the difference in wealth is the historical residential structural injustice discussed in chapter 3. The value of a family's household makes up about two-thirds of all family wealth.[40] Inheritance from generation to generation, in large part as a result of house values, is also an important reason for the disparity in wealth.[41] While laws and policies have worked together to restrict economic opportunities of African American people, they were and are designed to provide economic opportunities for people with economic resources, that is, mostly middle- and upper-middle-class white people.

> The reason Black people are so far behind now is not because of now. It's because of then.[42]
>
> —Clyde Ross

ECONOMIC AFFIRMATIVE ACTION FOR UPPER-CLASS PEOPLE

> The heart of racism was and is economic, though its roots are also deeply cultural, psychological, sexual, religious, and, of course, political. Due to 240 years of brutal slavery and an additional 100 years of legal segregation and discrimination, no area of a relationship between Black people and white people in the United States is free from the legacy of racism.
>
> —Jim Wallis, *America's Original Sin*

Home Mortgage Interest Deductions

Home mortgage interest deduction (HMID) allows home-owners to deduct the interest they pay on their mortgage and their real estate tax from their taxable income. It disproportionately helps people able to buy a house and those who buy high-value homes—mostly white people. High-income households (i.e., mostly white people) are also more likely to purchase second homes. So white people enjoy the most benefits of the HMID policy.

In 2015, the HMID saved taxpayers $71 billion, more than double the $29.9 billion that the government spent for housing for low-income households. Eighty-five percent of the savings go to high-income households and only 6 percent goes to low-income households. High-income earners (mostly white people) make up just 12 percent of households but receive 60 percent of federal housing assistance.[43]

When you look at a multimillion-dollar home on the beach or in a resort area, you probably don't realize that you are looking at real estate subsidized by the government, that is, handouts or affirmative action for mostly wealthy white people to buy bigger homes or second homes. The HMID is one of the largest tax breaks in the tax code. The White House estimates that it will cost the federal government $101 billion per year. For comparison, all federal spending on education programs will total around $70 billion.[44]

The IRS also gives a significant tax break to people when selling their homes because they don't have to pay tax on capital gains or on how much they earned because of the growth in value of their house. Half of the value of this tax break goes to those in the upper-income quintile, that is, mostly relatively wealthy white people.[45]

The other federal government law that provides economic housing assistance is Section 8 of the Housing Act. The federal government provides assistance to more than two million, mostly low-income people to help with rental and housing assistance. The total support for poor people in 2015 was $29.9 billion, that is, less than one-third of the $101 billion support provided to relatively wealthy people as a result of the HMID tax savings. For every dollar of the tax subsidy or savings from home mortgage interest deductions going to families in the bottom fifth of the income distribution, about $100 goes to those in the top fifth.[46] The pattern of homeownership and growing inequality in home values means that, in practice, the deduction is simply a gift-wrapped check from the federal government to the upper-middle-class, that is, mostly white people.[47]

529 Plan

Another "affirmative action" for mostly relatively wealthy white people is the federal government's 529 Plan. It gives a tax incentive to parents and grandparents to invest in their children's and grandchildren's education. Investors are normally required to pay taxes on interest earned from investments. With a 529 Plan, investors do not have to pay taxes on the amount of interest earned. For example, if a grandparent invested $5,000 in a child's education account from birth to age sixteen, the government would forego all of the taxes that would normally have to be paid on the interest earned for those sixteen years. The amount of tax dollars lost by the federal government or the amount essentially given to relatively wealthy white people by the government could be substantial. Because of significant income and wealth disparities, the great majority of African American people cannot afford to take advantage of this government handout. So the beneficiaries are mostly middle- to upper-income white people.

Retirement Programs

Another significant affirmative action program of the federal government to disproportionately help mostly wealthy white people is its tax policy regarding saving for retirement. Low-income people living paycheck to paycheck simply don't have money to make periodic payments to a retirement program. Upper-middle-class people can.

Here is how it works. Suppose you are able to invest $5,000 a year into your retirement plan and you are in the 20 percent tax bracket. You are able to deduct that $5,000 from your yearly taxable income, thereby saving $1,000 in taxes. Over time, your contribution will grow in value until you retire. You won't have to pay any taxes on the money that your savings has earned in all of those years. You will have to begin to pay taxes on the money you withdraw when you retire. By then, you will probably be in a lower tax bracket because you are not working. Each year, you will have saved money because you didn't have to pay taxes on the amount of your income that you were able to put into your plan. You will have also saved significantly because you would

125

not have had to pay taxes on all the profit you earned over the years. Over twenty or thirty years, that amounts to a tremendous savings.

The federal government annually foregoes more than $100 billion in personal income tax revenue due to the retirement savings incentives.[48] Another $20 billion in reduction in state taxes amounts to about $20 billion lost income revenue, according to an estimate of researchers at the New School.[49] In other words, the government has provided an affirmative action program to help relatively wealthy, mostly white people get richer.

Federal policies intended to expand opportunities for low-income families and communities for greater homeownership, retirement savings, economic investment, and access to college actually provide one-half of the $400 billion federal assistance to the top 5 percent of taxpaying households.[50] The bottom 20 percent of households received almost nothing. Black and Latino households were disproportionately among those receiving little or no benefits.

You may have heard of the theological concept of the "preferential option for the poor" referred to in liberation theology. That is, the gospel of Jesus is filled with stories of Jesus's love for those who suffer the most: poor and oppressed persons. Our government has created a tax policy of "preferential option for the wealthy," or policies diametrically opposed to gospel values of caring for the least of God's people. Politically, it would be a mortal sin for most politicians to advocate a change to the tax codes in ways that would require wealthy white people to forego their tax advantage and instead provide support for those in greatest need. This is, however, exactly what Jesus taught us to do: to advocate for poor people.

Long-term wealth accumulation of white people came from the labor of enslaved people and the slavery of convict labor as a result of the Black Codes. It came from sharecropping and exploitation of poorly paid African American workers who worked in the most dangerous jobs. It came from the Homestead Acts that gave 1.5 million white people land. It came from the good-paying union jobs provided by the government during World War II. It came from the New Deal policies that disproportionately helped

126

white people. It came from affirmative action tax policies that disproportionately benefitted white people.

Systematic and discriminatory government policies transferred wealth from the labor of African American people to corporations and financial institutions, that is, to mostly white people. Government policies helped white people move into the middle class and prevented African American people from moving into the middle class.

It took more than 150 years of slavery, Jim Crow, sharecropping, convict labor, segregation, and institutionalized discrimination in education, housing, and employment, along with control by way of the criminal justice system, laws, and government policy to work together to create the tremendous wealth gap that exists today between white people and African American people.

Immigrant European workers and their families have also been treated cruelly by corporations during our Industrial Revolution. Their labor has also "subsidized" the growth of our economy and transferred money to wealthy white people. But none suffered slavery nor the slavery of convict labor. None were controlled and separated by Jim Crow laws. All eventually were able to assimilate into the "melting pot." Only a relatively few African American people, however, were able to accumulate upper-middle-class and upper-class wealth to live the "American dream." The proof of the historic injustice is evident in the statistics that show the significant wealth and income gap between African American and white people.

INCOME DISPARITIES

Income is different from wealth. Income includes earnings from work, social security, and pension benefits and interest on savings and investments. It is analogous to a stream. It is the money received to get by day-to-day and week-to-week. Wealth is analogous to a pond. It is the value of what a family accumulates. It consists of the value of one's home, savings, car, and retirement investments minus one's debt. It is hard to put money from the stream into the pond if you live paycheck to paycheck.

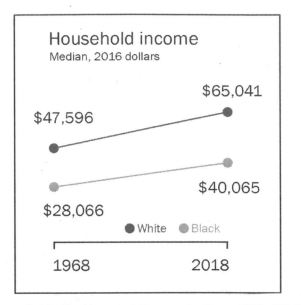

Figure 8: Median Household Income by Race, 1968–2016[51]

Wealth Disparities

As previously indicated, the median white family wealth is **forty-one times** more than the median wealth of African American families. The median African American family owns just over $3,500 in wealth compared to nearly $140,000 median white family wealth. Median wealth is a better representation of a typical family than average wealth since it avoids the upward pull of extremely high net-worth families.

The Urban Institute found that the white family's average wealth was more than **seven times** greater than the African American family's wealth.

The Institute for Policy Studies found that if the racial wealth divide is left unaddressed, median African American household wealth is on the path to hit zero by 2053 and the Latin American household wealth is projected to hit zero twenty years later.

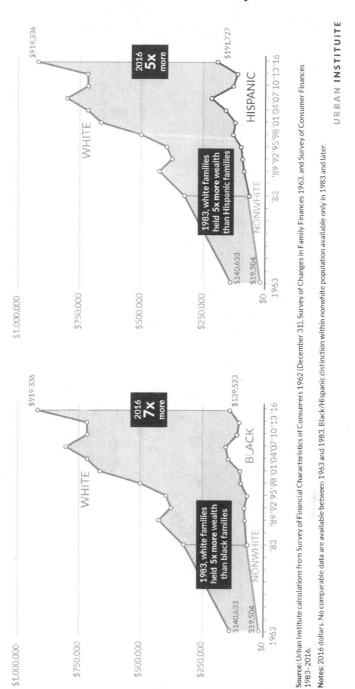

Figure 9: Average Family Wealth by Race or Ethnicity, 1963–2016[52]

Source: Urban Institute calculations from Survey of Financial Characteristics of Consumers 1962 (December 31), Survey of Changes in Family Finances 1963, and Survey of Consumer Finances 1983–2016.

Notes: 2016 dollars. No comparable data are available between 1963 and 1983. Black/Hispanic distinction within nonwhite population available only in 1983 and later.

URBAN **INSTITUTE**

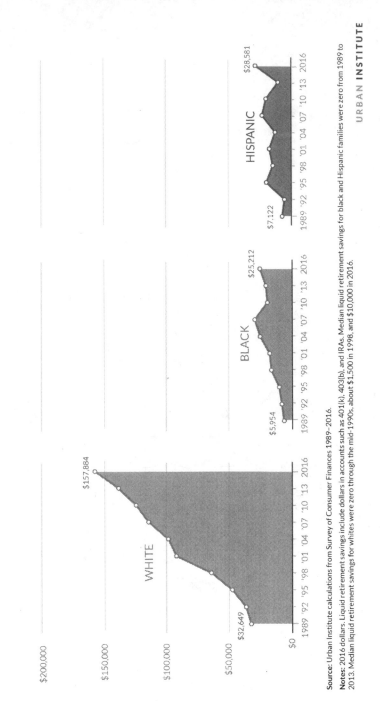

Source: Urban Institute calculations from Survey of Consumer Finances 1989–2016.

Notes: 2016 dollars. Liquid retirement savings include dollars in accounts such as 401(k), 403(b), and IRAs. Median liquid retirement savings for black and Hispanic families were zero from 1989 to 2013. Median liquid retirement savings for whites were zero through the mid-1990s, about $1,500 in 1998, and $10,000 in 2016.

Figure 10: Average Family Liquid Retirement Savings, 1989–2016[53]

Black and Hispanic families also have less money for retirement.

This disparity in wealth puts African American families at a *tremendous* disadvantage relative to white families who have significant wealth to provide for their families. Wealth provides a powerful stepping-stone on the path to economic success. For example, the wealth of parents and grandparents can provide money for such things as the following:

- tuition for a private education at preschool, kindergarten, elementary, high schools, colleges, and graduate schools for children and grandchildren
- enrichment expenditures for music lessons, art classes, dance lessons, sports camps, summer camps, SAT test-taking courses, and so on
- travel and other educational opportunities
- computers, books, and learning devices
- tutors and consultants for admission to universities
- emergencies such as healthcare costs; without resources to pay for an emergency, a family could lose its house and become homeless
- money to survive periods of unemployment and layoffs, which could also lead to homelessness
- money to buy a house or to help your children or grandchildren buy a house
- money to invest in a retirement plan
- money to start a business or help your child start a business
- inheritance to leave to children and grandchildren

THE INSIDIOUSNESS OF ECONOMIC DISCRIMINATION

Research has shown that there are many other ways that African American people are treated unfairly economically. A federal investigation of Adams Mark Hotel that began in July 1999 found that African American guests nationwide were forced to pay more than white people for comparable accommodations and were kept out of hotel restaurants and lounges because they were thought to be bad for business.[54] This type of insult was found by Harvard economic professor Sendhil Mullainathan to be one of many. He and Marianne Bertrand, an economist at the University of Chicago, mailed resumes to employers with job openings and measured which ones were selected for callback interviews. They randomly used stereotypically African American names (such as "Jamal") on some and stereotypically white names (like "Brendan") on the other. The same resume was roughly 50 percent more likely to result in callbacks for an interview if it had a "white" name. Mullainathan also reported that when whites and Blacks were sent to bargain for a used car, Blacks were offered initial prices roughly $700 higher, and they received far smaller concessions. *Professor Mullainathan said that he could go on and on with other examples of economic discrimination.*[55]

This vicious cycle has been going on for four hundred years and is being perpetuated today. It came about by deliberate discriminatory government policies that limited opportunities for wealth accumulation of African American people and provided economic opportunities for white people. Princeton professor Eddie S. Glaude Jr., in his book *Democracy in Black*, gives some insight into what this disparity in wealth means for African American people. He points out studies that show the following:[56]

- One in five African American children is growing up in extreme poverty. That child's parents make less than $11,746 per year for a family of four. They live on $979 per month; $226 per week; or $32 per day.
- In twenty-five of the fifty states and the District of Columbia, at least 40 percent of African American children are poor.
- Three in ten African American children grow up in poverty while only one in ten white children live in poverty.

Professor Glaude points out that this poverty crushes the dreams of millions of African American children. It almost ensures that they live less healthy lives, drop out of high school, experience some form of violence in their lifetime, and are more likely to be caught up in the criminal justice system. It means they will likely end up raising their children in the same horrifying conditions that they grew up in.[57]

AN OPEN DOOR—
SPORTS IN AMERICA

Of all of the areas of competition in America, such as achievement in education, job performance, academy awards, academic awards, and so on, there is none where performance can be measured so clearly as in sports. No one could deny the performance of Jesse Owens, Jackie Robinson, or Mohammad Ali. Because of their courage, the passage of the Civil Rights Act of 1964, and the courage of other athletes such as John Carlos, Tommy Smith, the Williams sisters, Jack Johnson, Jim Jeffries, Colin Kaepernick, Althea Gibson, Curt Flood, and many others, African American people have had the opportunity to participate on a level playing field in sports in recent years.

When barriers to discrimination in sports were lowered, the performance of African American athletes in basketball, football, track, and other sports became clear. When the doors of opportunity gradually opened, high school and college coaches, athletic directors, professional sports coaches, managers, and owners began to realize that, to win, they now had to have the best athletes, not just the best white athletes. This created a dramatic change in the complexion of sports in America at all levels except team ownership. Is it possible that the source of all this economic repression is because, deep down, many white people realize that if African American people are given equal opportunity altogether, many would excel and be significant competition in all areas of endeavor, just as they are in sports? Isn't fear the source of racism? Can you imagine what the face of America would look like today if, for the last 150 years, African American

133

people had been given equal opportunities and were measured on a fair competitive basis in education and all areas of employment, not only in sports?

Racism is a net that is cast widely and woven tightly. It is a vicious cycle. Lower home values in African American neighborhoods result in schools in those neighborhoods receiving less funding. Less funding means fewer resources and lower-paid teachers, which leads to education disparities in test scores and a poor education. A poor education results in fewer job opportunities, which leads to less income and few opportunities for travel, summer camp, theater, music lessons, computers, and so on. Little income means little access to health insurance and healthcare. It means no savings. So without savings and no family inheritance, the pond is empty. So there is no money to make mortgage payments to prevent foreclosure during periods of layoffs, unemployment, and medical emergencies. There is a risk of homelessness. There is no money for tuition, to start a new business, for retirement, or to help your children and grandchildren. This net has trapped African American people for centuries. The fault lies not in the "stars" or within African American people. The fault lies within the hearts of those who have designed and cast the net—the executive, legislative, and judicial branches of our government. The fault lies in those people who benefit from this injustice, who are "able to respond" to this injustice and just don't care.

APPLICATION

Catholic Social Teaching

Today in our country, men, women, and children are being denied opportunities for full participation and advancement in our society because of their race. The educational, legal, and financial systems, along with other structures and sectors of our society, impede people's progress and narrow their access because they are Black, Hispanic, Native American, or Asian. These structures of our society are subtly racist, for these structures reflect the values that society upholds. They are geared to the success of the majority and the failure of the minority.[58]

Reflection

1. Imagine how Jesus would feel about people who call themselves Christian and have designed these structures so that people like them have economic advantages over those with the greatest need.
2. Imagine how African American people would be living today if, over the last four hundred years, instead of implementation of policies that benefit white people and restrict opportunities of African American people, *all* of our doors of opportunity had been opened to everyone, not just sports, and we had lived up to our constitutional promise of treating all people equally.
3. Imagine how many more African American teachers, principals, MDs, PhDs, CEOs, business owners, bankers, judges, elected officials, government administrators, and so on we would have today if African American families had resources to pay or to help pay for a university education.
4. Imagine how successful African Americans would have been able to affect the lives of their family members and friends in the same way that successful white people have helped their family members and friends.
5. Imagine how much wealth African American people would have accumulated over the years if the government provided economic assistance equally to all people. Consider:

   - How many home foreclosures and resulting homelessness could have been avoided had African American people had economic resources to pay rent and mortgage payments, to survive layoffs, unemployment, temporary

disability from injury, and healthcare emergencies.
- How many more African American people would have been able to buy homes in safe neighborhoods.
- How many more African American people today would have savings in a retirement program.
- How many more grandparents would have been able to help pay for the education of their grandchildren.
- How many more African American people would have been able to move from toxic environments.
- How many more African American people would not have been imprisoned had they been able to pay a good criminal lawyer. How many heartaches would have been avoided.
- How many African American people would not have died needlessly had they been treated equally and had money to pay for health insurance.
- How many dreams of African American parents for their children could have been realized if African American people were treated fairly and equally.

Discussion

1. As you read this chapter, did you recognize any economic benefits you, your parents, your grandparents, or your ancestors received from government policies that benefit mostly white people?
2. How did you feel as you realized the extent of the economic advantage our government has given to white people and not to people of color?
3. Do you now have a better understanding of how people of color could think white people have privilege?

4. How do you imagine you would have felt reading this chapter if you were an African American person?

   - Would you have felt rejected by those in power?
   - Would you have felt resentment, alienation, frustration, and anger?
   - Would you have felt that you and yours are "owed" by the government?

Response

Are you and your family served by African American or Latin American people or other people of color, such as, landscapers, manicurists, pedicurists, home services, elder care, car cleaning, trash removal, food servers, or others? Think about these aspects:

1. Do you know if any of the people who serve you and your family are paid a fair wage?

   - Is there any way you could find out?
   - If they are not paid a fair wage, is there anything you could do?
   - Do those who serve your family have health insurance and workers' compensation insurance?

2. If you are a student, do you know if the people at your school who work in maintenance, security, and the cafeteria are paid fair wages with benefits including retirement programs and healthcare?

   - Is there a relationship between their wages and your tuition?
   - Are they unionized?
   - Have they ever tried to create a union?
   - Has the school ever tried to prevent workers from forming a union?

137

3. If you learned that the people serving you and your family were paid unfair wages, do you think, as a Christian, you have a responsibility to respond in any way?
4. Have you ever supported union workers in their struggles for justice?
5. If you are working, is your workforce integrated? If not, why not?

- Are people of color treated unfairly in any way?
- Are there unjust disparities in wages or benefits?
- Is there a fair balance of African American and white people at all levels of the hierarchy? If not, is there anything you could do about it?

Prayer Invitation

Abba, gather into your sacred heart all of the millionaires, legislators, government administrators, judges, CEOs, and others who have the power and resources to repair the economic injustice suffered by African American people. Transform their hearts and open their minds. Awaken in them your Holy Spirit of love, that they see and understand the tremendous imbalance in income and wealth created by these laws and policies from which they benefit and African American people suffer.

Grant them eyes to see and hearts to feel this injustice. Grant them wisdom and courage so that they do everything in their power to rescue those who are homeless and unemployed, those without healthcare, those mistreated by the criminal justice system, and all people who suffer from institutional violence created by structural injustice. *Abba*, protect the victims of this injustice. Grant them courage and strength. Grant them justice.

9

RESTORATIVE JUSTICE

REPARATIONS

Middle- and upper-middle-class white people did not create the structures of injustice that have so brutally oppressed, harmed, and continue to harm African American people. But they and their families are complicit to the extent that they participate in and are beneficiaries of this unjust system. They are responsible to the extent they are able to respond to injustice. However, individual responses to fight racism will not have much impact on the tremendous disparities that exist today. Only the people in power who have resources can make the significant change necessary to repair the harm caused by four hundred years of racism. The people in power are the judges, legislators, government officials and administrators at all levels, CEOs, small business owners, managers, supervisors, university presidents, labor leaders, police chiefs, and so on. But is it enough for our government to recognize the harm of racism and then pass laws and ensure that they are effectively implemented to treat all people equally? Roy L. Brooks tells this story:

> Two persons—one white, the other Black—are playing a game of poker. The game has been in progress for almost 400 years. One player—the white one—has been cheating during much of this time, but now announces: "From this day forward, there will be a new game with new players and no more cheating." Hopeful, but somewhat suspicious, the Black player

responds: "That's great. I've been waiting to hear you say that for 400 years. Let me ask you, what are you going to do with all those poker chips that you have stacked up on your side of the table all these years?" "Well," says the white player, somewhat bewildered by the question, "I'm going to keep them for the next generation of white players, of course."[1]

Beginning to play fairly, with significant advantage because of accumulated wealth, education, skills, and social contacts in a competitive society against players who are at tremendous disadvantage does nothing to restore or to mend the harm that was done. It does nothing to cause healing. If all we do is work together to try to change the rules and to ensure that they are enforced, as important as that work is, history tells us that there will likely be a backlash and, at best, there will be a slow process with very gradual changes. Those gradual changes have resulted in the structures of injustice still at play today.

There appears to be a significant awakening among white people today. A Monmouth University poll found that 71 percent of white people believe that racial injustice is a "big problem" in the United States.[2] This is up from 57 percent reported by the Kaiser Family Foundation in 2015.[3] However, Princeton professor Eddie S. Glaude Jr. reported that 60 percent of working-class white Americans believe that discrimination against whites is a bigger problem than discrimination against Blacks.[4]

So whether or not Americans have the collective will to eliminate structural injustice and repair the tremendous harm done to African American people is an open question. It will be answered by every person of power and every organization and every person of integrity. What is at stake for African American people is restorative justice. For white people, it is their souls:

O! had I the ability, and could reach the nation's ear, I would, today, pour out a fiery stream of biting ridicule, blasting reproach, withering sarcasm, and stern rebuke. For it is not light that is needed, but fire; it is not the gentle shower, but thunder. We need the storm, the whirlwind, and the earthquake. The feeling of the nation must be quickened; the conscience of the nation must be roused; the propriety of the nation must be startled; the hypocrisy of the nation must be exposed; and its crimes against God and man must be proclaimed and denounced. (Frederick Douglass, July 5, 1852) [5]

There can be no hope of reconciliation and redemption for the sin of racism without first recognizing and acknowledging our participation in an unjust racist system, that is, confession and apology. There can also be no hope of reconciliation and redemption without restorative justice. Authentic confession requires a "firm purpose of amendment," that is, to make it better. It's not enough to say, "I'm sorry. I won't do it again." Any confession or apology without steps taken to repair the harm done will not result in healing for the perpetrator or the victim. Atonement requires restorative justice.

To begin to understand how to make it better, in 2019, both the U.S. House of Representatives and Senate proposed to establish a commission to study and consider a national apology and proposal for reparations for slavery and discrimination and the impact of these forces on African American people today, and to make recommendations to Congress on remedies to repair this harm: Senate Bill 1083 and House Bill 40. For three decades, Congress refused to pass HR 40. Its drafter representative, John Conyers Jr., a Michigan Democrat and descendant of enslaved Americans, died in 2019—during the four-hundredth anniversary of the arrival of the first Africans enslaved in Virginia— without the bill ever making it out of committee.[6] Some of the injustices that these bills are meant to address are these:

- Approximately four million African American people and their descendants were enslaved in the United States and colonies that became the United States from 1619 to 1865.
- The slavery that flourished in the United States constituted an immoral and inhumane deprivation of Africans' life, liberty, African citizenship rights, and cultural heritage, and denied them the fruits of their own labor.

- Following the abolition of slavery, the U.S. government, at the federal, state, and local levels, continued to perpetuate, condone, and often profit from practices that continued to brutalize and disadvantage African Americans, including sharecropping, convict leasing, Jim Crow, redlining, unequal education, and disproportionate treatment at the hands of the criminal justice system.
- As a result of the historic and continued discrimination, African Americans continue to suffer debilitating economic, educational, and health hardships, including but not limited to having nearly one million Black people incarcerated; an unemployment rate more than twice the current white unemployment rate; and an average of less than one-sixteenth of the wealth of white families, a disparity that has worsened, not improved, over time.

Congress proposed that the commission study and recommend appropriate remedies that, among other issues, consider the following questions:

- How will the government offer a formal apology, that is, confession?
- How can federal laws and policies that continue to affect African Americans disproportionately and negatively as a group, and those that perpetuate the lingering effects, materially and psycho-socially, be *eliminated*?
- How can injuries suffered be reversed and appropriate policies, programs, projects, and recommendations be provided for the purpose of *reversing* the injuries?
- What form of compensation should be awarded, through what instrumentalities, and who should be eligible for such compensation?

- What other rehabilitation or restitution to African American descendants is warranted and what form and scope should those measures take?

If our representatives were to honor the Golden Rule embraced by virtually all religions of treating people the way they would like to be treated, there should be unanimous agreement to provide economic support to achieve the following:

- Remedy the imbalances in education by providing equal funding and significant support to help make up for historical injustices, including, as a minimum, free high-quality education including free university education.
- Provide economic support for affordable housing for African American people and other people of color.
- Significantly reform the criminal justice system and voters' rights and provide funds to remediate all environmental hazards, especially hazards in schools and lead hazards in homes.
- Provide healthcare for all African American people and everyone.
- Correct the imbalances in income and wealth by providing a living wage, adequate social security retirement benefits, small business loans, employment opportunities, and work programs that provide for full employment similar to those provided to mostly white people by the New Deal after the Great Depression.
- Raise the minimum wage to at least $15 per hour.
- Provide federal job guarantees to ensure everyone who is able to work has a job and is paid a living wage.

There will be much discussion by our representatives if there is to be agreement on the details of appropriate means and ways to pay for remedies. One way to obtain money would be to ask the wealthiest one-tenth of 1 percent of the people in the

United States, that is, those with household wealth of $20 million and above, to pay just 1 percent more annual taxes. According to the Institute for Policy Studies, a 1 percent increase would generate an estimated $1.899 trillion in revenue over ten years.[7] That would be a good start.

Other ways to obtain money for reparations include:

- Change our tax code to stop subsidizing the wealthy in so many ways and instead invest in opportunities for low-wealth families to build wealth.
- Tax capital gains as ordinary income. There is no justification for taxing capital gains at lower rates than we tax middle-class workers.
- Increase inheritance and estate taxes.

We could also get money by decreasing our military spending, which is about three times more than China and more than the combined spending of the seven next largest countries combined. Those members of Congress who honor the teachings of Jesus should recognize that spending needlessly on the military diverts revenue that could be used to repair the harm of racism.

> He shall judge between the nations,
>   and shall arbitrate for many peoples;
> they shall beat their swords into plowshares,
>   and their spears into pruning hooks;
> nation shall not lift up sword against nation,
>   neither shall they learn war any more.
>
> —Isaiah 2:4

Another way to reduce the wealth disparities would be the creation of Baby Bonds as proposed by Senator Cory Booker. The plan would give all newborns $1,000 and then give children of low-income households $2,000 each until the age of eighteen when it would have amounted to $46,000, that is, assuming a 3 percent rate of return. Only low-income families would receive $2,000 each year until the child is eighteen, that is, those with family income below the poverty line of $25,100. As family income increases, the amount received would gradually decrease until family income reaches $125,751, when it would receive nothing.

Naomi Zewde, a Columbia University postdoctoral researcher, estimated that in 2015, the median white person aged eighteen to twenty-five had a net worth of $46,000. The median Black person had a median net worth of $2,900. That is a ratio of 15.9 to 1. White young people were nearly sixteen times richer than their Black counterparts.

Zewde looked back and estimated what those eighteen- to twenty-five-year-olds would have as net worth had a Baby Bond policy been law at their birth. She found that in her model, which was similar to the model used by Senator Booker, the median white, young person would have had a net worth of $79,159. The median Black young person would have had a net worth of $57,845. A gap remains, but the ratio has been reduced to 1.4, almost eliminating the wealth gap.[8]

The United States is the richest country in history. It surely has the resources to significantly restore the harm caused by racism. So far, however, those in power have not opened their hearts to care enough to repair the harm caused by generations of racism. People who deny the injury that racism is causing today suffer a spiritual blindness. People who silently participate in its benefits and do nothing to combat the injustices suffer the moral injury. They suffer a closed heart that lacks understanding, compassion, wisdom, and love.

Healing of white people's spiritual injury requires confession, apology, and restorative justice. Healing can occur by advocating for reparations, organizing, participating with advocacy groups, standing with groups like Black Lives Matter, and speaking up when racist remarks are made. There are thousands of particular ways white people can respond to the evils of racism. Some of those ways can be found in the appendix, "Further Reading and Resources," which provides a list of books to understand and combat racism. One of the most powerful ways for transformation of one's heart to occur is by having personal contact and opportunities to learn something of another person's story, which is the topic of the next chapter.

APPLICATION

Catholic Social Teaching

Distributive justice at times requires *unequal* treatment to assuage morally relevant differences. Thus, strategies of "affirmative action" or "just opportunities" require the diligent attention of the Christian community. This notion is deeply rooted in the tradition of the preferential option for poor people that permeates the Hebrew Testament, in particular. This reality is fully recognized in the Pontifical Council for Justice and Peace 2001 document, "Contribution to World Conference Against Racism, Racial Discrimination, Xenophobia, and Related Intolerance."[9]

Reflection & Discussion

1. Before you read this book, had you ever heard a white person advocate for reparations for African American people?
2. Had you been in favor of economic reparations for African American people?
3. If you were an African American person, do you think you would be in favor of reparations?
4. Has your opinion regarding reparations changed?

    • If so, how? Why?

5. What do you think is the most compelling reason that the government should make changes to restore some measure of economic justice for African American people?
6. Do you think there are compelling reasons why government should not change any policy to benefit African American people?

Response

1. Do you know any of your congressional representatives' position on reparations?

2. Would you be willing to contact your congressional representatives to encourage them to support Senate Bill 1083 and House Bill 40?
3. If you heard a person arguing that there is no need for reparations, would you likely respond? How?
4. Have you ever thought of contributing to the Unite Fund to support scholarships for African American students or to support other organizations such as the Southern Poverty Law Center?

Prayer Invitation

Abba, I beg you to grant me the grace to recognize opportunities to get to know African American people and people of color better. Grant me the courage to respond to opportunities that you provide for me to get to know African American people and other people of color better. Grant me the grace of your wisdom so that I see and care for all people as precious reflections of you. Grant me opportunities to get to see you more clearly and to love you more dearly.

10

THE POWER OF STORY

A heavy and cruel hand has been laid upon us. As a
people, we feel ourselves to be not only deeply injured,
but grossly misunderstood. Our white countrymen do not
know us. They are strangers to our character, ignorant
of our capacities, oblivious to our history and progress,
and are misinformed as to the principles and ideas that
control and guide us as a people. The great mass of
American citizens estimates us as being a characterless
and purposeless people; and hence, we hold up our heads,
if at all, against the withering influence of a nation's scorn
in contempt.

—Frederick Douglass, National Colored Convention,
Rochester, New York, 1853

Jesus told us that the kingdom of God is within us all. We are
sacred. We are temples of God's Holy Spirit of Jesus. We are all
that precious. His message was simple:

Love one another.
Treat others the way you would like to be treated.
Care for the sick and the lame, the lepers, the women
    abused,
the mentally ill, the bereaved mothers,
the orphans, and the despised.
The least will be first.
The exalted will be humbled;

148

the humble will be exalted.
Those rejected are the cornerstone.
Blessed are the meek, the poor in spirit, those who mourn,
and those who seek justice and peace.

Jesus's message emphasized the dignity of all people and that we are all worthy of respect. His message was about loving and caring for one another, especially those rejected and oppressed by the dominant culture. One way to begin to understand and care for oppressed people is to get to know the names of those you meet every day. It is a simple thing to call a person by her or his name. James Baldwin titled one of his books *Nobody Knows My Name*, apparently because he was overlooked by white people so often. Knowing a person's name and getting to know something of his or her story is *key* to growing in understanding, compassion, and love. People become "real" to us when we know their name, their children's names, what they love, their hopes and dreams, their talents and struggles, their sense of humor, what has broken their hearts, and especially how they have been harmed by bigotry and racism. We can learn of a person's story through books, movies, plays, poetry, and music. But what is most powerful is the personal encounter with the other. When we know the other person's story, his or her life can "touch" us. It takes courage to step out of your comfort zone and into the camp of the "other." Sherine Green has done it many times.

SHERINE'S STORY

I grew up in Clarendon, a small rural community in central Jamaica about an hour's drive from the capital, Kingston, an area of beautiful mountains, rivers, streams, and plains. However, the people are some of the poorest people on the island. They cry out to God through music—reggae—the inspiration and spirituality of the people. Music is their therapy: songs such as "Linstead Market" and "Redemption Song" by Bob Marley, or "Many Rivers to Cross" by Jimmy Cliff. Our music conveys the tremendous strength of a people who struggle in so many ways. Even in times of desperation, the Jamaican people sing and dance.

In our farming parish known for the best oranges, bananas, sugar, and fine rum, I would often see the farm workers who travel to and from the United States each year for work. I also saw many impoverished people who were sick.

I lived next door to a major hospital. It was one of the best and yet lacked in resources. I began to see and hear the cries of poor people. I also learned that part of our culture was to help those in need, to share food, and to speak up for the oppressed.

"Emancipate yourselves from mental slavery."

Traveling through rural Jamaica, you can't help but see the poorest of poor people, mostly Black, some of whom are desperate. The white people all seemed to be doing well. Any child of color will tell you that white people seem more blessed. The missionaries who came were white. The fairytale books we read portrayed the white people with the greatest advantages. Some children and families even try to be white by bleaching their skin. Class and color ruled.

I remember listening to the music of reggae and ska (a Jamaican forerunner of reggae) and hearing these words: "Emancipate yourselves from mental slavery." I wondered for many years why Black people needed to be emancipated. I would soon come to realize that Black people were still being enslaved by systems of oppression.

I was an early reader. I read of the struggle of Black people in other countries. I made the connection between colonialism, stolen wealth, impoverishment of African people, and its relationship to European economic growth. I recognized how white supremacy has historically injured people of color by robbing them of their wealth and dignity by people who thought they were superior. As I got older, I could see more clearly how color and class plagued the Jamaican society. People of mixed heritages who were lighter had a better chance to get the best jobs and attend the best schools. I also witnessed the great faith of Black Jamaicans.

I also remember the many times I went with my grandmother to shop in the market. The vendors would share stories of traveling for hours and being unable to sell their potatoes or carrots because there were so many other vendors. I remember the times we would walk by a poor vendor because we could not buy from everyone. It hurt as a child to see a poor widow right in front of me desperate to sell her produce. I could see and feel her tears. I became even sadder if the vendor we walked away from was a child my age.

Witnessing the suffering of poor people made a great impression on me as a child. In the United States, we don't get to see the farm workers who gather the bananas we eat or the beans for our coffee and those who provide other food for our tables. We don't get to see the impoverished women who work in the factories to provide us with our clothing. So we are unaware of the struggles of those who feed and clothe us and provide us with so many other consumer goods. We are not touched by their suffering.

At the same time that I was witnessing the suffering poor in my own community, I was beginning to be more aware of the suffering of people of color elsewhere. Everyone in Jamaica who had a TV watched American TV. Since we didn't have a TV, I went to my cousin's house. He sold Singer TVs and had one. Many people would sit and watch the shows. I remember seeing white families with lush lawns and beautiful homes. It seemed that wealth, privilege, and whiteness went hand-in-hand. I remember wondering why Black folks were not portrayed in the same way as white people. I was beginning to understand that Black people were suffering even in a great country like the United States.

My parents hoped I would be a medical doctor, climb the social ladder, and perhaps help them too. I was determined to see the world and arise from poverty. My hope was to make my family proud of me in every way, shape, and form I could. My mother and father worked very hard so I could attend a private high school. My mother worked two jobs. She, like many Jamaican women, also migrated to work for a wealthy British expat family in the Cayman Islands. I lived with my grandmother. Many Jamaican people worked as babysitters, chefs, and gardeners and provided other services for mostly white families. Many of my Jamaican friends are doing well today because of the tremendous sacrifices made by their parents who left their families and migrated to take care of white people's families in Europe, the United States, and Canada, or in our case, the Caymans. They did the best they could.

Toronto, Canada

During my first year in college, I was invited to accompany a small group from my diocese in Jamaica to see Pope John Paul II during his visit to Toronto, Canada. This was a dream come true. I always wanted to visit North America. We stayed with a host family in Mississauga, a suburb of Toronto. We met people of different races and lifestyles from all over the world.

Many of the recent immigrants to Toronto are people of color who are poor and live in segregated areas. I saw as I did in Jamaica that the affluent people were mostly white people. Those who had to struggle to get along were mainly people of color. I began to recognize the unjust systems and to wonder what I could do about these injustices. I was also beginning to understand the reason for the disparities between people of color and white people. It did not have to do with who had the best work ethic or was the most intelligent. It had to do with the institutions that supported white people at the expense of people of color. It had to do with white supremacy.

Newcastle, Northern Ireland

The next opportunity I had to leave Jamaica and live in a white community was when I received an award from the Jamaican Theological Seminary where I was studying counseling. I accompanied a small group of seminarians to visit the city of Newcastle, a small community just outside of Belfast in Northern Ireland. The purpose of the visit was to bring together seminarians from Jamaica and families of Newcastle to share experiences and get to know each other and, in the process, learn something of reconciliation and faith and the power of learning another person's story.

In Northern Ireland, the problem was not alienation because of skin color. It was alienation because of the separation between Catholics and Protestants. Our group consisted of young Protestant men and women seminarians. I was the only Catholic. We spent time playing games and sports, talking to each other, listening to reggae music, and praying together. We shared our faith experiences.

The children constantly asked about our culture, the color differences in Jamaica, and our songs. Most of the seminarians were simple people who had never left their small town in Jamaica. The encounter resulted in a profound impact on all of us. At the end of our stay, the mothers, fathers, children, and seminarians embraced with many tears. Fifteen years later, many still keep in touch with the children and families they met in Newcastle. What I learned was that within the cultural exchange rooted in the encounter, we begin to gradually see the "other" person as sister or brother.

Brooklyn, New York

I then had another opportunity to live with white people in Brooklyn, New York. I spent one year as a Mercy volunteer living in an intentional community created by the Sisters of Mercy. I lived with five young white women from upper-class families. Our community was built on the principles of simplicity, spirituality, and service. The participants were recent college graduates, teachers, counselors, physical therapists, and others. I served as a child development specialist to assess the needs of children in foster care, mostly children of color. I helped as best I could but often just spent time being present and witnessing people's journeys. Some of my work included visiting the projects, prisons, and group homes for teenagers and simply playing with children. One of the most difficult things I experienced was seeing children forcibly removed from their home and put in foster care. It was heartbreaking.

I had many opportunities to connect with people and to listen to their stories. At the end of the day, we had time to reflect on the many eucharistic moments of grace we experienced through our encounters. The experiences in Brooklyn made clear to me the tremendous differences between Black and white communities that I knew. As a woman of color, I could identify the suffering and pain carried by other people of color. The privilege of being white became so much clearer. I also saw how privilege can cause blindness to what others suffer. But most important, I saw how serving in another culture and learning another's story is mysteriously and deeply transformative.

Romero Center—Camden, New Jersey

My experience in Brooklyn led me to the Romero Center in Camden, New Jersey, one of the most impoverished cities in the United States. I developed and participated in retreats for high school and college students and adults. The participants were mostly middle- and upper-middle-class white people who spent a week or a weekend meeting and serving the people of Camden, mostly people of color. They served in homeless shelters, nursing homes, schools, soup kitchens, and other places. At the end of each day, they reflected on the gospel values of Jesus, Catholic social teaching, and how they had been "touched" by interacting with the people of Camden.

I was now in a position where I could be, in the words of Oscar Romero, "a microphone for justice." I served as a bridge to connect white people from the suburbs, who had little understanding of the impact of racism, with the people of Camden. I listened to many participants who, at the end of the day, shared their experiences. It was a blessing to witness the powerful effect the encounters had on participants.

I remember a high school student from the upper east side of Manhattan who, after witnessing the injustices in Camden, was so moved as to eventually serve in one of the most impoverished housing projects in New York. I remember a business major from Villanova University saying that he was so touched serving a family in a project that he wanted to change his major. He asked my advice. I suggested he complete his degree and perhaps find a way to teach financial literacy and money management to low-income families. He was so delighted to see how he could use his talents to serve those in need. He is just one example. Almost all the participants at the Romero Center seemed to have been changed by their experience of getting to know the "other." I still keep in touch with some of the retreatants who are now serving in marginalized communities. I was blessed to be witness to the mystery of their transformation.

While at the Romero Center, I also lived in an intentional community, Camden House, with a group of white middle- and upper-middle-class university-educated young people. All were familiar with Catholic social teaching. Our goal was to fight institutionalized racism, especially the environmental racism suffered by people in South Camden. We lived in an area where we could smell the stench of industrial and human waste every day. We lived in solidarity with the people in South Camden. We advocated for justice. We got to know our neighbors.

We invited the children to play in our backyard where we had a garden and a greenhouse. We encouraged them to dream and believe that the sky was the limit. It wasn't easy. There were dreadfully scary moments. At times, I felt disconnected from both groups. My prayer life became more important. We had hoped to change Camden for the better. Our experience changed us for the better.

Christ Our Light—Cherry Hill, New Jersey

Now in 2020, I am working at Christ Our Light Parish in Cherry Hill, New Jersey, as the director of youth faith formation. I direct programs for youth from seventh through twelfth grades as well as young adults. We provide opportunities for youth to serve in Camden. We also invite the children of Camden to spend time with us in Cherry Hill: playing, picnicking, eating ice cream, and praying together. The children from Camden are always grateful as we are too for every smile, handshake, and hug. We invite young people from Camden to join our mission trip to Jamaica, and we invite speakers from churches in Camden to speak to our parishioners to share their gifts and testaments of faith.

Jamaica

For several years, I have led small groups of parishioners, mostly white upper-class people, adults and children, to spend a week serving mentally and physically challenged children in Jamaica. Our intention is that through the encounter, the participants begin to connect their understanding of the presence of Jesus in the Eucharist with the Holy Spirit of Jesus residing in the "least" of us. When we arrive, we are met with the outstretched arms of Jesus as the children reach out and welcome us.

We spend time listening to the stories of the children and staff and learning something of Jamaican culture, folk songs, and dances. We read Scripture and pray together. The most powerful moments come after we have wiped away our tears of pity and simply played with the children, many of whom have profound disabilities. Some of the most touching experiences occur as we feed the children as we are fed with the spiritual nourishment of grace, which opens our hearts. Our young people always leave with hearts wounded and opened by the children. I remember comments such as "they are so nice" and "they are just like us" and, even better, "I want to do this again."

I am convinced that the key to growing in love and compassion of oppressed people is by having the courage to leave a familiar, safe environment and to enter into a relationship with those who suffer injustice. That is how hearts are broken open in love. I have seen miraculous transformations occur within me in Toronto, Canada, and within the seminarians in Newcastle, Northern Ireland; within the participants at the Romero Center and in Jamaica; and within my roommates in Brooklyn and Camden and the parishioners of Christ Our Light.

It takes courage, but that's how the magic occurs.

> There is one elemental truth, the ignorance of which kills countless ideas and splendid plans: The moment one definitely commits oneself, then Providence moves, too. All sorts of things occur to help one that never otherwise would have occurred....
> Whatever you can do or dream you can do, begin it. Boldness has genius, power, and magic in it. Begin it now.
>
> —Goethe

VINCE'S STORY

I grew up in a white working-class area of Philadelphia. Just about everyone in my neighborhood was racist. My grammar school, Immaculate Conception, was 99 percent white. Just across the street was Pastorius, a public school with many African American students. We were never told as much, but we all thought that our school was better and that we were better. The seeds of white supremacy were planted in our young brains just as they are planted in all of us.

My high school, Cardinal Dougherty, was also segregated. We didn't realize it, but most of my high school friends and I would have correctly been called bigots. After high school, I started at LaSalle University as the civil rights movement was making news. The "times they were a-changing," as Bob Dylan reminded us in song.

The mission of the Christian Brothers at LaSalle University was to educate the working class. Every course was rooted in issues of social justice. The brothers reinforced the gospel values we learned from the Immaculate Heart sisters. I learned to never forget my roots. I watched Sydney Poitier movies and sang Harry Belafonte songs. I didn't think I treated people differently because of their race. I thought I was color-blind.

Just as I had practically no understanding of African American culture, I simply had no understanding of Latin American people. I had never met a person from Latin America. After I graduated from college, I served in the Peace Corps. I lived in a poor community in Maracaibo where I had many experiences with Venezuelan people, both very poor and middle class. I learned the language and enjoyed the food, music, and politics. I fit in. I was immersed in the culture and became part of it.

I eventually focused on a career in worker injury and disease prevention. My work took me to Lima, Peru, where I served with the United Nations International Labor Organization. I lived in Lima with my wife and three children and eventually worked in eight countries in Latin America. I grew to love the Latin American people and their various cultures.

Still, even with these cross-cultural experiences, I had little understanding of how the seeds of racism toward African American people were embedded in me until I served for about ten days in Haiti with the Missionaries of Charity at the House of the Destitute and Dying in Port-au-Prince. I gave foot and back massages to men who were close to death. I also witnessed frail men, themselves dying, who were feeding and caring for others who needed help. By the gift of grace, I felt no pity. I just felt love and respect. Gradually my eyes, mind, and heart were opening. A whole new world was opening.

Since my first trip to Haiti about twenty years ago, I have returned each year to serve with the Missionaries of Charity: to hold and feed children close to death, suffering from diseases related to malnutrition. Most are nurtured back to health. Some suffering from tuberculosis and AIDS don't make it.

I have been in the company of hundreds of mothers whose children were at risk of death from easily preventable diseases related to malnutrition. Witnessing their love and distress was heartbreaking. I have also had the privilege of serving African American people living with AIDS at Calcutta House in Philadelphia by practicing reflexology, a healing therapy akin to foot massage. Those experiences and other experiences of serving the needs of other people of color broke my heart many times and gradually opened it more and more to all people of color. I now feel the same love for African American people as I have of Latin American people. I am *sure* it is because of God's grace given during the intimate encounters I had with people in Latin America, Haiti, Philadelphia, and Camden. I am also sure that the key to white people's awakening to their blindness and inability to really see and care for people of color is by having opportunities to be in touch with and intimately knowing the stories of people of color. It is really simple. Understanding of others is essential to growing in love.

Solidarity

Understanding another person's story opens hearts and leads to solidarity. Solidarity is a key concept of Catholic social thought. Pope John Paul II defined solidarity as a *"firm and persevering determination* to commit oneself to the common good, that is to say to the good of all, and each individual, because we are all really responsible for all."[1]

Solidarity is an expression of compassion. It results from the relationship we have with the "other." The "other" ceases to be other when the other person becomes friend.

> Without the cultivation of solidarity—rooted in lament, compassion, and transformative love—truth-telling and affirmative redress results in superficial palliatives that leave the deep roots of injustice undisturbed.
> —Bryan N. Massingale, *Racial Justice and the Catholic Church*

If we stay in our own "gated communities" and fail to form relationships with people oppressed, we will likely be numb, unconcerned, and indifferent to the suffering caused by racism. It takes going out into the camp of the "other" to get to know the story of the person oppressed. That is how hearts are broken open. That is how transformational love is born—when the two become one. That is how the Word becomes flesh and we truly understand the meaning of Eucharist—when we truly feel the unity of God's Holy Spirit of Jesus in the compassion we have for our friend.

APPLICATION

Catholic Social Teaching

As Catholics, we are called to listen and know the stories of our brothers and sisters. We must create opportunities to hear, with open heart, the tragic stories that are deeply imprinted on the lives of our brothers and sisters, if we are to be moved with empathy to promote justice.[2]

Reflection & Discussion

1. Who is the African American person that you know best?

   • How did you meet?
   • How did you get to know her or him?

2. How many African American people do you know
   fairly well? How did you get to know them?
3. Are there African American people that you see on
   a regular basis? Do you know their names?
4. Have you ever had personal encounters with
   people of color because you were serving the needs
   in their community?

   - Do you remember how you felt before you
     arrived?
   - How did the people you met or served respond
     to you?
   - How did you feel about the encounter after you
     left?
   - Did it take some courage to enter the camp of
     the other?
   - Was it worth it?
   - What did you learn?
   - Would you do it again?
   - Did you do something like that again?
   - Did it change you in any way?

Response

1. Do you have any desire to go on a mission trip to
   serve in an impoverished area in the United States
   or another country?

   - If so, do you know where that desire comes
     from?
   - Is there anything holding you back?

2. Do you know any ways to enter into communication
   with people of color to learn or serve?

   - Does your school provide opportunities to visit
     and serve in impoverished communities?
   - Does your church reach out to people living
     nearby in impoverished areas?

- Do you know of any ways you could get to know your African American friends better?
- Have you ever thought of visiting and worshiping at a predominantly African American church?
- Have you ever thought of mentoring through Big Brothers Big Sisters?
- Can you think of any other ways you could get to know the stories of people of color?

Prayer

Abba, open my eyes to see you residing in all people. Break my heart open so that I love and have compassion for the imprisoned, those suffering addictions, homeless people, abused children and women, people who are hungry, mentally ill people, and those who are sick and dying.

I beg you to grant me the grace to see all people, especially those who suffer the most, as clearly as I see my own mother and father and all of my loved ones. Grant me the opportunity to get to meet you, to know your name, to know your story, to humbly serve your needs, to bring about the kingdom of love here on earth.

11

REPAIRING THE WOUNDED HEART

> I strongly suspect that if we saw all the difference even
> the tiniest of our prayers to God make, and all the
> people those little prayers were destined to affect, and
> all the consequences of those effects down through the
> centuries, we would be so paralyzed with awe at the
> power of prayer that we would be unable to get off of our
> knees for the rest of our lives.
>
> —Peter Kreeft

THE POWER OF PRAYER

Some people get knocked off their horses and awaken. For most, it is a very gradual process. For Thomas Merton, a Trappist monk, it happened after years of prayer, when he was "suddenly" given the grace to really "see" people at an intersection in Lexington, Kentucky. We too, through persistence, faith, and prayer, can make ourselves more receptive to God's grace, to be able to see the kingdom of God before us.

Jesus told us that we should seek, knock, and ask God for what we really want. He told us that prayer can move mountains. When Jesus was asked, "How should we pray?" he told us to pray that God's kingdom of love manifests here on earth as in heaven. So if Jesus is right, God will respond to our prayers and our desire to love and serve just as any loving parent would. We just have to ask—not for good weather, or to pass a test, but rather for God to respond to our desires for justice, healing, forgiveness, and mercy, and for greater love—that God's kingdom comes alive here on earth.

> You must want like a God.
> —Thomas Traherne, seventeenth-century Anglican mystic

If we persist and sincerely beg God for the grace to love more, for opportunities to serve and be instruments in bringing about God's kingdom of love, God will surely respond. God can't help but respond to such prayers as the following:

> *Abba*, I beg you with all my heart to grant me the grace to see with Jesus's eyes, to hear with his ears, to love with his heart, and to understand with his mind.
> Open my eyes so that I see you more clearly, love you more dearly, and follow you more nearly.
> Inflame my heart with your love for poor persons and for the poverty in everyone.
> Make me a channel of your love.
> Grant me the grace of Jesus's peace, kindness, love, humility, wisdom, and courage.
> Come, Holy Spirit of Jesus, alive in my heart.
> I love you, I love you, I love you. Increase my love for you and everyone.
> Open my heart, *Abba*, open my eyes.

Centering Prayer

Centering prayer can help us "be still." The more still we are, the more present we are. The more present we are, the more clearly we can see. Each day we could go to a quiet place at a time when there are no distractions and light a candle or put on some meditation music. Sit straight, relax, and begin to watch the rhythm of your breath. Breathe naturally. Then remember that you are in the presence of God.

You could imagine breathing the light of the Holy Spirit into your spiritual heart in the center of your chest and feel it permeate every cell through your body to your fingers and toes. As you breathe out, you can imagine being showered and surrounded by the radiant light of the Holy Spirit—God in you and you in God.

Some can visualize easier than others. It is not necessary at all. We can just breathe and let ourselves be seen by God. Edwina Gateley has put the experience very simply and beautifully in her poem "Let Your God Love You":

> Let Your God
> Love You.
> Be Silent.
> Be Still.
> Alone.
> Empty.
> Before your God
> Say nothing.
> Ask nothing.
> Be silent.
> Let your God
> Look upon you.
> That is all.
> God knows.
> God understands.
> God loves you
> With an enormous love,
> And only wants
> To look upon you
> With that love.
> Quiet.
> Still.
> Be.
> Let your God—
> Love you.

In centering prayer, we don't try to attain or achieve any particular state. We don't try to make ourselves still or to seek some level of awareness or experience. It is about surrendering and letting go. We let go of expectations and outcomes and make ourselves available to God by becoming receptive. It is about opening our heart, not our thoughts.

In a matter of time, our mind will wander. When it does, we simply say a mantra to center ourselves and come back to the awareness of God's Holy Spirit in our breath and in us. "Come, Holy Spirit," "Jesus," "I'm yours," "Mary," "Abba," or any other short word or phrase can be used to bring back our awareness of God's presence. Then we follow our breath again until the next thought comes to mind. Instead of thinking about the distraction, how long we were distracted, what caused our distraction, or blaming ourselves for being distracted, we note our awareness of the distraction and realize that we have just been called back by God. Then we say our mantra and without further thought go back to sitting in the presence of God.

Centering prayer enables us to become more "still"—more present. Through grace, it enables our heart to open. As our heart gradually opens, we begin to see more clearly—people become more REAL. In the beloved British children's story *The Velveteen Rabbit*, the stuffed rabbit asks the wisest and oldest toy in the nursery, the Skin Horse, "What is REAL?"

> "Real isn't how you are made. It is a thing that happens to you. When a child loves you for a long, long time, not just to play with, but REALLY loves you, then you become REAL."
>
> "Does it hurt?" asked the Rabbit.
>
> "Sometimes," said the Skin Horse, for he was always truthful.
>
> "Does it happen all at once, like being wound up?"
>
> "It doesn't happen at once," said the Skin Horse. "You become. It takes a long time. That's why it doesn't happen often to people who break easily, or who have sharp edges, or who have to be carefully kept. Generally, by the time you are Real, most of your hair has been loved off and your eyes drop out and you get loose in the joints and very shabby. But these things don't matter at all because once you are Real, you can't be ugly, except to people who don't understand."

Through God's grace, as we get to know and understand more African American people, our heart gradually opens more and more and they become REAL. As your heart opens, you will naturally become inclined to care for and pray for those suffering addictions, their loved ones, people who are sick and dying, those imprisoned and their loved ones, and the homeless, and that God's love transforms the hearts of those who control the power to reverse these injustices. You will also be more likely to respond to opportunities to fight racism and speak out when necessary.

We can also pray for the forgiveness of all people, including ourselves, who have consciously or unconsciously harmed other people. We can beg for mercy and understanding for us all, especially those of us who are in greatest need.

Belief that God hears and responds to every prayer is key. So too is persistence. If our faith is shallow, we can pray for greater faith. We can pray at any time—while driving, for each person we pass as we walk along the street, while we are waiting in line at the store, before we sleep, when we awaken during the night, and in the morning.

Just about every day you will hear of or read about an African American person suffering an injustice related to racism. You will always find opportunities to be an instrument of God's love through prayer and to shower God's love on African American people and all who suffer injustices of all types. As your heart opens more and more, you will find more and more opportunities to serve the needs of those suffering injustice and neglect—more opportunities to be an instrument of God's love in bringing about God's kingdom, right here before us—right here within us all.

Prayer to Mary

Mary, friend and mother of all
through your Son, God has found a way
to unite himself to every human being, called to be one
    people, sisters and brothers to each other.

Repairing the Wounded Heart

We ask for your help in calling on your Son, seeking
     forgiveness for the times when
we have failed to love and respect one another.
We ask for your help in obtaining from your Son
the grace we need to overcome the evil of racism
and to build a just society.
We ask for your help in following your Son, so that
     prejudice and animosity
will no longer affect our minds or hearts
but will be replaced with a love that respects
the dignity of each person.
Mother of the Church, the Spirit of your Son Jesus
warms our heart;
Pray for us.[1]

APPENDIX

Further Reading and Resources

COMBATING RACISM

The most practical and comprehensive book that we found was *Uprooting Racism: How White People Can Work for Racial Justice* by Paul Kivel, 4th revised and updated edition. We also recommend *How to Be an Antiracist* by Ibram X. Kendi.

This appendix provides a list of other books on ways to combat racism and a list of books that provide a greater understanding of racism.

> *A Little Book of Race and Restorative Justice: Black Lives, Healing and US Social Transformation* (The Little Books of Justice and Peacebuilding) by Fania Davis
>
> *Diversity beyond Lip Service: A Coaching Guide for Challenging Bias* by La'Wana Harris
>
> *Guide for White Women Who Teach Black Boys* by Eddie Moore, Ali Michael, and Marguerite W. Penick-Parks
>
> *How We Fight White Racism* by Kenrya Rankin and Akiba Solomon
>
> *Interpreting Racism* by Rebecca Adkins and Alishia Oglesby
>
> *It's Time to Talk (and Listen): How to Have a Constructive Conversation about Race, Class, Sexuality, Ability and*

Gender in a Polarized World by Anastasia S. Kim, PhD, and Alice Del Prado, PhD

Little Book of Dialogue for Difficult Subjects: A Practical Hands-On Guide by Lisa Schirch

Little Book of Restorative Discipline for Schools by Rhonda McGee

Little Book of Restorative Justice for Colleges and Universities, revised and updated edition, by David Karp

Little Book of Restorative Justice for People in Prisons by Barb Toews

Little Book of Restorative Justice in Education: Fostering Relationships, Healing, and Hope in Schools by Katherine Evans and Dorothy Vaandering

Me and White Supremacy: Combat Racism, Change the World, Become a Good Ancestor by Layla F. Swaad

Not Light, But Fire: How to Lead Meaningful Race Conversations in the Classroom by Matthew R. Kay

Teaching Race: How to Help Students Unmask and Challenge Racism by Stephen Brookfield

The Racial Healing Handbook: Practical Activities to Help You Challenge Privilege, Confront Systemic Racism and Engage in Collective Healing by Anneliese A. Singh, PhD, LPC

UNDERSTANDING RACISM

America's Original Sin: Racism, White Privilege, and the Bridge to a New America by Jim Wallis

Blind Spot by Mahzarin R. Banaji and Anthony G. Greenwald

Courageous Conversations about Race by Glen Simpleton

Eloquent Rage: A Black Feminist Discovers Her Superpower by Brittany Cooper

Appendix

Everyday Anti-Racism: Getting Real about Race in Schools edited by Mica Pollack

Good White People by Shannon Sullivan

How to Be Less Stupid about Race: On Racism, White Supremacy, and the Racial Divide by Crystal Fleming

How We Fight White Supremacy by Akiba Solomon and Kenrya Rankin

I'm Still Here: Black Dignity in a World Made for Whiteness by Austin Channing Brown

Inner World of Racial Justice: Healing Ourselves and Transforming Our Communities through Mindfulness by Rhonda McGee

Interpreting Racism by Rebecca Adkins and Alicia Oglesby

Mindful of Race: Transforming Racism from Inside Out by Ruth King

Racial Dharma by Jasmine Syedullah, Lama Rod Owens, and Angel Kyodo Williams

So You Want to Talk about Race by Ljeoma Oluo

Tell Me Who You Are: Sharing Stories about Race, Culture, and Identity by Winona Guo and Preya Vulchi

The Executed God: The Way of the Cross in Lockdown America, revised and expanded edition, by Mark Louis Taylor

The Memo: What Women of Color Need to Know to Secure a Seat at the Table by Minda Harts

The Perils of "Privilege": Why Injustice Can't Be Solved by Accusing Others of Advantage by Phoebe Haltz Bovy

We Want to Do More Than Survive: Abolitionist Teaching and the Pursuit of Educational Freedom by Bettina L. Love

What Does It Mean to Be White: Developing White Racial Literacy by Robin DiAngelo

White Awake: An Honest Look at What It Means to Be White by Daniel Hill

White Kids: Growing Up with Privilege in a Racially Divided America (Critical Perspectives on Youth, Book 1) by Margaret A. Hagerman

Why I'm No Longer Talking to White People about Race by Reni Eddo-Lodge

Books by Tim Wise:

Affirmative Action: Race Preference in Black and White

Culture of Cruelty

Dear White America

I Don't See Color

Speaking Treason Fluently: Anti-Racial Reflections from an Angry White Male

Under the Affluence

White Lies Matter

White Like Me

"Black Voices, Black Stories"

Another wonderful resource is Xfinity voice remote. Just say, "Black Voices, Black Stories" into your TV remote control and you will have access to the following:

- **Learning More:** Listen and learn about the contemporary fight for justice and equality
- **Understanding More:** Films and documentaries on the history of racial discrimination
- Voices of the Civil Rights Movement
- Bold movies to make you think
- **Shows to start the conversation:** TV shows that help change the narrative and spark conversation

Appendix

- Supporting Black-owned media and other Black content providers
- How to discuss race with kids
- Hearing from thought leaders
- How to support the Black community

NOTES

INTRODUCTION

1. Thomas Merton, *Conjectures of a Guilty Bystander* (New York: Doubleday, 1966), 140–42.

2. Kenneth G. Davis, OFM, Conv., and Leopoldo Pérez, OMI, eds., *Preaching the Teaching: Hispanics, Homiletics, and Catholic Social Justice Doctrine* (Scranton, PA: University of Scranton Press, 2005), 27.

CHAPTER 1: THE BACKLASH TO THE END OF SLAVERY

1. Equal Justice Institute (EJI), *Lynching in America: Confronting the Legacy of Racial Terror*, 3rd ed. (Montgomery, AL: Equal Justice Institute, 2017), 10–11; based in part on Henry Lewis Gates, *Stoney the Road: Reconstruction, White Supremacy, and the Rise of Jim Crow* (New York: Penguin Press, 2019).

2. T. W. Gilbreth, "The Freedmen's Bureau Report on the Memphis Race Riot of 1866" (May 22, 1866); as reported in EJI, *Lynching in America*, 9.

3. Jennifer Rae Taylor, "Constitutionality Unprotected: Prison Slavery, Felon Disenfranchisement, and the Criminal Exception to Citizens' Rights," *Gonzaga Law Review* 47, no. 2 (2011–12): 365, 374; as reported in EJI, *Lynching in America*, 23.

4. James G. Hollandsworth Jr., *An Absolute Massacre: The New Orleans Race Riot of July 30, 1866* (Baton Rouge: Louisiana State University Press, 2001), 3, 104–5, 126; Donald E. Reynolds,

"The New Orleans Riot of 1866, Reconsidered," *Louisiana History: The Journal of the Louisiana Historical Society* 5, no. 1 (Winter 1964): 5–27; as reported in EJI, *Lynching in America*, 9.

5. Charles Lane, *The Day Freedom Died: The Colfax Massacre, the Supreme Court, and the Betrayal of Reconstruction* (New York: Henry Holt and Company, 2008), 266, estimated that the massacre left between sixty-two and eighty-one Black people dead; as reported in EJI, *Lynching in America*, 12.

6. Thomas Howell, "The Colfax Massacre: An Essay Review," *Louisiana History: The Journal of the Louisiana Historical Society* 51, no. 1 (Winter 2010): 69; as reported in EJI, *Lynching in America*, 22.

7. Eric Foner, *Reconstruction: America's Unfinished Revolution; 1863–1877* (New York: Harper & Row, 1988), 530n11; as reported in EJI, *Lynching in America*, 13.

8. Alan W. Trelease, *White Terror: The Ku Klux Klan Conspiracy in Southern Reconstruction* (New York: Harper & Row, 1970), 3, 5; as reported in EJI, *Lynching in America*, 14.

9. Trelease, *White Terror*, 113–15n33; James G. Dauphine, "The Knights of the White Camelia and the Election of 1868: Louisiana's White Terrorists; A Benighting Legacy," *Louisiana History: The Journal of the Louisiana Historical Society* 30, no. 2 (Spring 1989): 173; see also Foner, *Reconstruction*, 425n11; as reported in EJI, *Lynching in America*, 14.

10. David M. Chalmers, *Hooded Americanism: The History of the Klu Klux Klan*, 3rd ed. (Durham, NC: Duke University Press, 1987), 18n53; Foner, *Reconstruction*, 428–29n11; as reported in EJI, *Lynching in America*, 15.

11. Lisa Cardyn, "Sexualized Racism/Gendered Violence: Outraging the Body Politic in the Reconstruction South," *Michigan Law Review* 100, no. 4 (February 2002): 675, 763; as reported in EJI, *Lynching in America*, 15.

12. Cardyn, "Sexualized Racism/Gendered Violence," 765, 768–69; as reported in EJI, *Lynching in America*, 15.

13. Eddie S. Glaude Jr., *Democracy in Black: How Race Still Enslaves the American Soul* (New York: Crown Publishers, 2016).

14. Glaude, *Democracy in Black*, 40–41.

15. Glaude, *Democracy in Black*, 41.

Notes

16. Douglas A. Blackmon, *Slavery by Another Name: The Re-Enslavement of Black Americans from the Civil War to World War II* (New York: Anchor Books, 2008); as reported in Paul Kivel, *Uprooting Racism*, 3rd ed. (Gabriola Island, Canada: New Society Publishers, 2017), 110, 111.

17. Blackmon, *Slavery by Another Name*, 297.

18. EJI, *Lynching in America*, 23.

19. EJI, *Lynching in America*, 40.

20. "Tulsa Race Riot," A Report by the Oklahoma Commission to Study the Race Riot of 1921 (February 28, 2001).

21. James H. Cone, *The Cross and the Lynching Tree* (Maryknoll, NY: Orbis Books, 2010), 6.

22. Harvey Young, "The Black Body as Souvenir in American Lynching," *Theatre Journal* 57, no. 4 (December 2005): 639–40; as reported in EJI, *Lynching in America*, 33.

23. Michael Norton and Samuel R. Sommers, "Whites See Racism as a Zero-Sum Game that They Are Now Losing," *Perspectives on Psychological Science* 6, no. 3 (2011): 215–18.

24. Bianca DiJulio et al., "Survey of Americans on Race," Kaiser Family Foundation/CNN (November 2015), https://files.kff.org/attachment/report-survey-of-americans-on-race.

25. Leon F. Litwack, *Trouble in Mind: Black Southerners in the Age of Jim Crow* (New York: Alfred A. Knopf, 1998), 281; Dora Apel, *Imagery of Lynching: Black Men, White Women, and the Mob* (New Brunswick, NJ: Rutgers University Press, 2004), 22; as reported in EJI, *Lynching in America*, 35.

26. Young, *The Black Body as Souvenir*, 639–40; as reported in EJI, *Lynching in America*, 35.

27. EJI, *Lynching in America*, 61.

28. "Racial Violence in the United States Since 1660," BlackPast.org, accessed April 23, 2021, https://www.blackpast.org/special-features/racial-violence-united-states-1660/.

29. Zinn Education Project, Teaching People's History, "Massacres in U.S. History Archives," Washington, DC, accessed April 23, 2021, https://www.zinnedproject.org/collection/massacres-us/.

30. Leon F. Litwick, *Been in the Storm So Long: The Aftermath of Slavery* (New York: Random House, 1979) 172–74, 284n166; as reported in EJI, *Lynching in America*, 68.

31. Nikole Hannah-Jones, "What Is Owed," *New York Times Magazine* (June 26, 2020).

32. See https://www.statista.com/statistics/585152/people-shot-to-death-by-us-police-by-race/.

33. Cone, *The Cross and the Lynching Tree*, xiv–xv.

CHAPTER 2: THE BACKLASH TO THE CIVIL RIGHTS MOVEMENT

1. Jim Crow refers to a song-and-dance caricature performed by Thomas D. Rice who blackened his face and ridiculed African American people.

2. Michelle Alexander, *The New Jim Crow: Mass Incarceration in the Age of Colorblindness* (New York: The New Press, 2012), 37.

3. Alexander, *The New Jim Crow*, 4.

4. PEW Center on the States, *One in 100: Behind Bars in America 2008* (Washington, DC: PEW Charitable Trusts, 2008), 5; as reported in Alexander, *The New Jim Crow*, 6.

5. U.S. Department of Health and Human Services, Substance Abuse and Mental Health Services Administration, "Summary of Findings from 2000 National Household Survey on Drug Abuse," *NHSAD Series H-13*, DHHS Pub. No. SM 01-3549 (Rockville, MD: 2001); as reported in Alexander, *The New Jim Crow*, 99.

6. Human Rights Watch, "Punishment and Prejudice: Racial Disparities in the War on Drugs," *HRW Reports* 12, no. 2 (2000); as reported in Alexander, *The New Jim Crow*, 7.

7. Paul Street, *The Vicious Circle: Race, Prison, Jobs, and Community in Chicago, Illinois, and the Nation* (Chicago: Chicago Urban League, Dept. of Research and Planning, 2002); as reported in Alexander, *The New Jim Crow*, 7.

8. Donald Braman, *Doing Time on the Outside: Incarceration and Family Life in Urban America* (Ann Arbor: University of Michigan Press, 2004), 3; citing D.C. Department of Corrections data for 2000; as reported in Alexander, *The New Jim Crow*, 7.

9. Marc Mauer and Ryan King, *A 25-Year Quagmire: The "War on Drugs" and Its Impact on American Society* (Washington, DC: Sentencing Project, 2007), 3; as reported in Alexander, *The New Jim Crow*, 60.

10. Howard N. Snyder and Melissa Sickman, "Juvenile Offenders and Victims: 2006 National Report," U.S. Department of Justice, Office of Justice Programs, Office of Juvenile Justice and Delinquency Prevention (Washington, DC: 2006); as reported in Alexander, *The New Jim Crow*, 99.

11. National Institute on Drug Abuse, "Monitoring the Future, National Survey Results on Drug Use, 1975–1999," vol. 1, *Secondary School Students* (Washington, DC: National Institute on Drug Abuse, 2000); as reported in Alexander, *The New Jim Crow*, 99.

12. National Institute on Drug Abuse, "Monitoring the Future," as reported in Alexander, *The New Jim Crow*, 99.

13. National Institute on Drug Abuse, "Monitoring the Future," as reported in Alexander, *The New Jim Crow*, 99.

14. U.S. Department of Health, *National Household Survey on Drug Abuse, 1999* (Washington, DC: Substance Abuse and Mental Health Services Administration, Office of Applied Studies, 2000), table G on 71; as reported in Alexander, *The New Jim Crow*, 99.

15. National Institute on Drug Abuse, "Monitoring the Future," as reported in Alexander, *The New Jim Crow*, 99.

16. Marc Mauer and Ryan S. King, *Schools and Prisons: Fifty Years After* Brown v. Board of Education (Washington, DC: Sentencing Project, 2004), 3; as reported in Alexander, *The New Jim Crow*, 98.

17. Human Rights Watch, "Punishment and Prejudice," as reported in Alexander, *The New Jim Crow*, 100.

18. Mauer and King, *A 25-Year Quagmire*, 2, 3; as reported in Alexander, *The New Jim Crow*, 60.

19. PEW Center on the States, *One in 100*; data analysis is based on statistics for mid-year 2006, published by the U.S. Department of Justice in June 2007; as reported in Alexander, *The New Jim Crow*, 100.

20. Human Rights Watch, "Punishment and Prejudice," as reported in Alexander, *The New Jim Crow*, 98.

21. Alexander, *The New Jim Crow*, 112.

22. Eileen Poe-Yamagata and Michael A. Jones, *And Justice for Some: Differential Treatment of Youth of Color in the Justice System* (Washington, DC: Building Blocks for Youth, 2000); as reported in Alexander, *The New Jim Crow*, 118.

23. Alexander, *The New Jim Crow*, 114.

24. Alexander, *The New Jim Crow*, 48.

25. Willard M. Oliver, *The Law & Order Presidency* (Upper Saddle River, NJ: Prentice Hall, 2003), 127–28, citing Dan Baum, *Smoke and Mirrors: The War on Drugs and the Politics of Failure* (Boston: Little, Brown, 1996), 13; H. R. Haldeman, *The Haldeman Diaries* (New York: G. P. Putnam's Sons, 1994), 53 (emphasis in original); as reported in Alexander, *The New Jim Crow*, 44.

26. John Ehrlichman, *Witness to Power: The Nixon Years* (New York: Simon and Schuster, 1970), 233; as reported in Alexander, *The New Jim Crow*, 44.

27. Ehrlichman, *Witness to Power*; as reported in Alexander, *The New Jim Crow*, 44.

28. Kevin Phillips, *The Emerging Republican Majority* (New Rochelle, NY: Arlington House, 1969); as reported in Alexander, *The New Jim Crow*, 45.

29. Thomas Byrne Edsall and Mary D. Edsall, *Chain Reaction: The Impact of Race, Rights, and Taxes on American Politics* (New York: Norton, 1992), 164; as reported in Alexander, *The New Jim Crow*, 49.

30. Alexander, *The New Jim Crow*, 52.

31. Alexander, *The New Jim Crow*, 53.

32. Katherine Beckett, *Making Crime Pay: Law and Order in Contemporary American Politics* (New York: Oxford University Press, 1997), 53; citing Executive Office of the President, Budget of the U.S. Government (1990); as reported in Alexander, *The New Jim Crow*, 49.

33. Jeff Dietrich, "Declaring a Cease Fire in the Drug War," *Catholic Agitator*, August 2009; as reported in Jeff Dietrich, *Broken and Shared: Food, Dignity, and the Poor on Los Angeles' Skid Row* (Los Angeles: Maryknoll Institute Press/TSEHAI Publishers, 2011), 379.

34. Alexander, *The New Jim Crow*, 181.

35. Dan Levin, "As More Mothers Fill Prisons, Children Suffer a 'Primal Wound,'" *New York Times*, December 29, 2019, 12.

36. Alexander, *The New Jim Crow*, 158.

37. Rachel L. McLean and Michael D. Thompson, *Repaying Debts* (New York: Council of State Governments Justice Center, 2007); as reported in Alexander, *The New Jim Crow*, 155.

38. Alexandra Natapoff, *Punishment without Crime* (New York: Basic Books, 2018).

39. 42 U.S.C. § 608(a)(9)(A) (forbidding assistance to "any individual who is violating a condition of probation"); Rebekah Diller et al., *Criminal Justice Debt: A Barrier to Reentry* (New York: Brennan Center for Justice, 2010), 28n202–4; 21 J.S.C. § 862; as reported in Natapoff, *Punishment without Crime*, 30.

40. Ezekiel Edwards, Will Bunting, and Lynda Garcia, *The War on Marijuana in Black and White* (New York: American Civil Liberties Union, 2013), 47, 48, 58; as reported in Natapoff, *Punishment without Crime*, 153.

41. Natapoff, *Punishment without Crime*, 153.

42. Investigation of the Ferguson Police Department (2015), U.S. Department of Justice, Civil Rights Division; as reported in Natapoff, *Punishment without Crime*, 152.

43. J. Kelly Lowenstein, "Crunch Time: Black People and Jaywalking in Champaign," *Chicago Tribune*, August 21, 2012; Topher Sanders et al., "Walking While Black: Jacksonville's Enforcement of Pedestrian Violations Raises Concerns that It's Another Example of Racial Profiling," *ProPublica and the Florida Times–Union*, November 16, 2017; Investigation of the Ferguson Police Department (2015), 4; as reported in Natapoff, *Punishment without Crime*, 153.

44. Investigation of the Ferguson Police Department (2015); as reported in Natapoff, *Punishment without Crime*, 153.

45. Investigation of the Ferguson Police Department (2015); as reported in Natapoff, *Punishment without Crime*, 153.

46. Human Rights Watch, "Punishment and Prejudice"; as reported in Alexander, *The New Jim Crow*, 7.

CHAPTER 3: RESIDENTIAL SEGREGATION

1. "Dr. King's Dream Denied: Forty Years of Failed Federal Enforcement; 2008 Fair Housing Trends Report," National Fair Housing Alliance, April 8, 2008, https://nationalfairhousing .org/wp-content/uploads/2017/04/2008_fair_housing_trends _report.pdf.

2. Richard Rothstein, *The Color of Law: A Forgotten* History of How Our Government Segregated America (New York: Live Right Publishing, 2017), 44.

3. Rothstein, *The Color of Law*, 63.

4. Rothstein, *The Color of Law*, 64.

5. Rothstein, *The Color of Law*, 64.

6. Rothstein, *The Color of Law*, 84.

7. Rothstein, *The Color of Law*, 79.

8. Jason Laughlin, "Racist Deeds Kept Real Estate from Non-White Owners," *Philadelphia Inquirer*, December 30, 2019, 1–2.

9. Rothstein, *The Color of Law*, 79.

10. Rothstein, *The Color of Law*, 80.

11. Rothstein, *The Color of Law*, 80.

12. Rothstein, *The Color of Law*, 103.

13. Rothstein, *The Color of Law*, 104.

14. Rothstein, *The Color of Law*, 105.

15. Rothstein, *The Color of Law*, 105.

16. Rothstein, *The Color of Law*, 106.

17. Rothstein, *The Color of Law*, 62.

18. Rothstein, *The Color of Law*, 31.

19. Rothstein, *The Color of Law*, 35–36.

20. Rothstein, *The Color of Law*, 95.

21. Rothstein, *The Color of Law*, 95.

22. Rothstein, *The Color of Law*, 96.

23. Rothstein, *The Color of Law*, 144.

24. Rothstein, *The Color of Law*, 144.

25. Rothstein, *The Color of Law*, 147.

26. Rothstein, *The Color of Law*, 150.

27. Rothstein, *The Color of Law*, 141.

28. Rothstein, *The Color of Law*, 141–42.

29. Vincent Hughes, "Redlining Is Still Keeping Homeownership Away from Minorities," *Philadelphia Inquirer*, May 7, 2018.

30. Troy McMullen, "The 'Heartbreaking' Decrease in Black Ownership," *Washington Post*, February 28, 2019.

31. Matthew Desmond, "White Hoods," *New York Times Magazine* (September 27, 2020).

32. "Brothers and Sisters to Us," U.S. Catholic Bishops (1979).

CHAPTER 4: SEGREGATION IN EDUCATION

1. Gary Orfield and Erica Frankenberg, with Jongyeon Ee and John Kuscera, "Brown at 60—Great Progress, a Long Retreat and an Uncertain Future," The Civil Rights Project (May 15, 2014).

2. Gary Orfield and Chungmei Lee, "Historical Reverses, Accelerating Resegregation, and the Need for New Integration Strategies: A Report of the Civil Rights Project," UCLA (August 2007), 9.

3. Orfield and Lee, "Historical Reverses," 3.

4. Orfield and Lee, "Historical Reverses," 3.

5. U.S. Department of Education, National Center for Education Statistics, Common Core of Data (CCD), Public Elementary/Secondary School Universe Survey Data. Data prior to 1991 obtained from the Analysis of the Office of Civil Rights data in Gary Orfield, *Public School Desegregation in the United States, 1968–1980* (Washington, DC: Joint Center for Political Studies, 1983); as reported in "Brown at 60," 11.

6. Sean F. Reardon, Elena Grewal, Demetra Kalogrides, and Erica Greenberg, "Brown Fades: The End of Court-Ordered School Desegregation and the Resegregation of American Public Schools," *Journal of Policy Analysis and Management* 31, no. 4 (Fall 2012), first published July 3, 2012.

7. Dana Goldstein and Anemona Hartocollis, "Prosecutors in California Say District Setup Purposefully Segregated Schools," *New York Times*, August 10, 2019.

8. Willis D. Hawley, "Who Knew? Integrated Schools Can Benefit All Students," *Education Week* 23, no. 34 (May 5, 2004): 4.

9. Barbara Laker, Wendy Ruderman, and Dylan Purcell, "Toxic City—The Ongoing Struggle to Protect Philadelphia's Children from Environmental Harm," *The Philadelphia Inquirer/Daily News*, Toxic City Series, May 2018.

10. Mary Filardo, Jeffrey M. Vincent, Ping Sung, and Travis Stein, "Growth and Disparity—A Decade of U.S. Public Schools Construction," in *Building Educational Success Together (BEST)* (October 2006): 16, http://www.21csf.org/csf-home/publications/BEST-Growth-Disparity-2006.pdf.

11. Filardo et al., "Growth and Disparity," 1.

12. Filardo et al., "Growth and Disparity," 2.

13. Filardo et al., "Growth and Disparity," 2.

14. Filardo et al., "Growth and Disparity," 2.

15. Filardo et al., "Growth and Disparity," 2.

16. Mark Schneider, "Do School Facilities Affect Academic Outcomes?"; as reported in Filardo et al., "Growth and Disparity," 3.

17. Jack Buckley, Mark Schneider, and Yi Shang, "Los Angeles Unified School District Facility and Academic Performance" (January 2004); as reported in Filardo et al., "Growth and Disparity," 30.

18. Glen I. Earthman, "Prioritization of the 31 Criteria for School Building Adequacy" (Baltimore: American Civil Liberties Union Foundation of Maryland, 2004); as reported in Filardo et al., "Growth and Disparity," 4.

19. "Ending School Overcrowding in California: Building Quality Schools for All Children," A Report from PolicyLink and MALDEF (Oakland, CA: PolicyLink, 2005), 4.

20. Jack Buckley, Mark Schneider, and Yi Shang, "The Effects of School Facility Quality on Teacher Retention in Urban School Districts" (Washington, DC: National Clearinghouse for Educational Facilities, 2004), 4.

21. Buckley, Schneider, and Shang, "The Effects of School Facility Quality," 30.

22. "Linking School Facility Conditions to Teacher Satisfaction and Success," ERIC Publication, ED480552 (Washington, DC: National Clearinghouse for Educational Facilities, 2003), 30.

23. Brian D. Smedley, Adrienne Y. Stith, Lois Colburn, and Clyde H. Evans, "The Right Thing to Do, the Smart Thing to Do: Enhancing Diversity in Health Professions," in *Summary of the Symposium on Diversity and Health Professions in Honor of Herbert W. Nickens, MD* (Washington, DC: National Academies Press, 2001).

24. National Center for Educational Statistics, Race and Ethnic Enrollment, "Indicator 6: Elementary and Secondary Education," last updated February 2019, accessed April 30, 2021, https://nces.ed.gov/programs/raceindicators/indicator_rbb.asp.

25. Department of Education, Office of Civil Rights, 2011–2012 School Year, accessed April 30, 2021, https://ocrdata.ed.gov/estimations/2011-2012.

26. Howard Witt, "School Discipline Tougher on African Americans," *Chicago Tribune*, September 25, 2007, http://www.chicagotribune.com/chi-070924discipline-story.html.

27. "Reclaiming the Promise: A New Path Forward on School Discipline Practices," American Federation of Teachers (October 20, 2018), 2, https://www.aft.org/position/school-discipline.

28. Witt, "School Discipline Tougher on African Americans."

29. American Civil Liberties Union, "School-to-Prison Pipeline," accessed April 30, 2021, https://www.aclu.org/issues/juvenile-justice/school-prison-pipeline/school-prison-pipeline.

30. "School Discipline," The Department of Education, Office of Civil Rights, Coalition of Schools Educating Boys of Color, accessed April 30, 2021, http://www.coseboc.org/policy/school-discipline.

31. "A First Look: 2013–2014 Civil Rights Data Collection," U.S. Department of Education Office of Civil Rights, issued June 7, 2016; revised October 28, 2016.

32. Bryan N. Massingale, *Racial Justice and the Catholic Church* (Maryknoll, NY: Orbis Books, 2010), x, xii.

CHAPTER 5: HEALTHCARE DISPARITIES

1. *Focus Newsletter*, March 21, 2003; as reported in Dr. Augustus A. White III, *Seeing Patients* (Cambridge, MA: Harvard University Press, 2011), 221.

2. Kara Gavin, "ACA Helped Make Health Insurance Access More Equal, but Racial and Ethnic Gaps Remain" (March 4, 2020), https://labblog.uofmhealth.org/industry-dx/aca-helped-make-health-insurance-access-more-equal-but-racial-and-ethnic-gaps-remain#:~:text=5%3A00%20AM-,ACA%20Helped%20Make%20Health%20Insurance%20Access%20More%20Equal,Racial%20and%20Ethnic%20Gaps%20Remain&text=Just%20before%20the%20ACA's%20insurance,of%20white%20adults%20under%2065.

3. Kaiser Family Foundation Fact Sheet about Uninsured Population (San Francisco: December 2018).

4. Institute of Medicine of the National Academies, *U.S. Health in International Perspective: Shorter Lives, Poorer Health* (Washington, DC: The National Academies Press, 2013), 2.

5. Linda Villarosa, "'A Terrible Price': The Deadly Racial Disparities of COVID-19 in America," *New York Times*, April 29, 2020.

6. Brian Smedley, Adrienne Stith, and Alan Nelson, eds., *Unequal Treatment: Confronting Racial and Ethnic Disparities in Health Care* (Washington, DC: Institute of Medicine, The National Academies Press, 2003); as reported in White, *Seeing Patients*, 212.

7. Willie J. Parker, "Black-White Infant Mortality Disparity in the U.S.: A Social Litmus Test," *Public Health Reports* 118 (July–August 2003): 336–37; as reported in White, *Seeing Patients*, 212.

8. Smedley, Stith, and Nelson, eds., *Unequal Treatment*; as reported in White, *Seeing Patients*, 212.

9. Knox H. Todd et al., "Ethnicity and Analgesic Practice," *Annals of Emergency Medicine* 35, no. 1 (January 2000): 11–16; as reported in White, *Seeing Patients*, 212.

10. Smedley, Stith, and Nelson, eds., *Unequal Treatment*; as reported in White, *Seeing Patients*, 212.

11. Smedley, Stith, and Nelson, eds., *Unequal Treatment*; as reported in White, *Seeing Patients*, 211.

12. Smedley, Stith, and Nelson, eds., *Unequal Treatment*; as reported in White, *Seeing Patients*, 211.

13. Donald A. Barr, *Health Disparities in the United States* (Baltimore: Johns Hopkins University Press, 2015), 229; emphasis added.

14. Gus Wezcrek, "Racism's Hidden Toll," *New York Times*, August 16, 2020.

15. Dayna Owen Matthew, *Just Medicine: A Cure for Racial Inequality in American Healthcare* (New York: New York Press, 2015).

16. California News Reel, "How Racism Impacts Pregnancy Outcomes," as reported in Cristina Novoa and Jamila Taylor, "Exploring African Americans' High Maternal and Infant Death Rates," Center for American Progress (February 1, 2018), https://www.americanprogress.org/issues/early-childhood/reports/2018/02/01/445576/exploring-african-americans-high-maternal-infant-death-rates/.

17. Jamila Taylor, "Racism, Inequality, and Health Care for African Americans," The Century Foundation (December 19, 2019), https://tcf.org/content/report/racism-inequality-health-care-african-americans/?agreed=1.

18. "Pregnancy Mortality Surveillance System," Centers for Disease Control and Prevention, accessed May 3, 2021, https://www.cdc.gov/reproductivehealth/maternalinfanthealth/pmss.html.

19. H. M. Eltoukhi, M. N. Modi, M. Weston, A. Y. Armstrong, and E. A. Stewart, "The Health Disparities of Uterine Fibroid Tumors for African American Women: A Public Health Issue," *American Journal of Obstetrics and Gynecology* 210, no. 3 (2014): 194–99, https://www.ncbi.nlm.nih.gov/pmc/articles/PMC3874080/#:~:text=indication%20for%20hysterectomies.-,Disproportionate%20Impact%20of%20Fibroids%20in%20African%20Americans,factors%20(1%2C5).

20. A. T. Geronimus, "The Weathering Hypothesis and the Heart of African American Women and Infants: Evidence and Speculation," *Ethnicity and Disease* 2, no. 3 (1992): 207–21; as reported in "Black Women's Maternal Health: A Multifaceted Approach to Addressing Persistent and Dire Health Disparities," Issue Brief, National Partnership for Women and Families (April 2018), https://www.nationalpartnership.org/our-work/health/reports/black-womens-maternal-health.html.

21. Emily E. Petersen et al., "Racial/Ethnic Disparities in Pregnancy-Related Deaths—United States 2007–2016," *Morbidity and Mortality Weekly Report* 68, no. 35 (September 6, 2019): 762–65.

22. A. Creanga, C. J. Berg, C. Syverson, K. Seed, F. S. Bruce, and W. Calahan, "Pregnancy-Related Mortality in the United States, 2006–2010," *Obstetrics and Gynecology* 125, no. 1 (2015): 5–12; A. Creanga, C. J. Berg, C. Syverson, et al., "Racial and Ethnic Disparities in Severe Maternal Morbidity: A Multi-State Analysis, 2008–2010," *American Journal of Obstetrics and Gynecology* 210, no. 5 (May 1, 2014); as reported in New York City Department of Health and Mental Hygiene, "Severe Maternal Morbidity in New York City, 2008–2012" (2016), https://www1.nyc.gov/assets/doh/downloads/pdf/data/maternal-morbidity-report-08-12.pdf.

23. New York City Department of Health and Mental Hygiene, Bureau of Maternal, Infant, and Reproductive Health, "Pregnancy-Associated Mortality: New York City, 2006–2010" (2015), https://www1.nyc.gov/assets/doh/downloads/pdf/ms/pregnancy-associated-mortality-report.pdf.

24. New York City Department of Health and Mental Hygiene, "Pregnancy-Associated Mortality," 6.

25. Rita Giordano, "Zip Codes Show Life Expectancy," *Philadelphia Inquirer*, December 18, 2018.

26. Giordano, "Zip Codes Show Life Expectancy."

27. Donald A. Barr, *Health Disparities in the United States: Social Class, Race and the Social Determinants of Health*, 3rd ed. (Baltimore: Johns Hopkins University Press, 2019), 227.

28. U.S. Department of Health and Human Services, Office of Minority Health, "Heart Disease and African Americans," updated 2018, accessed May 3, 2021, https://minorityhealth.hhs.gov/omh/browse.aspx?lvl=4&lvlid=19%20.

29. U.S. Department of Health and Human Services Office of Minority Health, "Stroke and African Americans," updated 2018, accessed May 3, 2021, https://minorityhealth.hhs.gov/omh/browse.aspx?lvl=4&lvlid=28.

30. U.S. Department of Health and Human Services, "Stroke and African Americans."

31. Kyndaron Reinier, Gregory A Nichols, Adriana Huertas-Vazquez, et al., "Distinctive Clinical Profile of Blacks Versus Whites Presenting with Sudden Cardiac Arrest," *Circulation* 132, no. 5 (2015): 380–87, originally published July 20, 2015.

32. Reinier et al., "Distinctive Clinical Profile of Blacks," 380–87.

33. Risa Lavizzo-Mourey and David Williams, "Being Black Is Bad for Your Health," *U.S. News & World Report*, April 14, 2016, https://www.usnews.com/opinion/blogs/policy-dose/articles/2016-04-14/theres-a-huge-health-equity-gap-between-whites-and-minorities.

34. U.S. Department of Health and Human Services, Office of Minority Health, "Asthma and African Americans," https://minorityhealth.hhs.gov/omh/browse.aspx?lvl=4&lvlid=15.

35. U.S. Department of Health and Human Services, "Asthma and African Americans."

36. U.S. Department of Health and Human Services, "Asthma and African Americans."

37. U.S. Department of Health and Human Services, "Asthma and African Americans."

38. American Cancer Society, "Cancer Facts and Figures for African Americans 2019–2020," accessed May 3 2021, https://www.cancer.org/research/cancer-facts-statistics/cancer-facts-figures-for-african-americans.html.

39. Lucas W. Thornblade, Susanne Warner, Laheh Melstrom, et al., "Association of Race/Ethnicity with Overall Survival among Patients with Colorectal Liver Metastasis," *JAMA Network Open* 3, no. 9 (September 9, 2020), https://jamanetwork.com/journals/jamanetworkopen/fullarticle/2770282?utm_campaign=articlePDF&utm_medium=articlePDFlink&utm_source=articlePDF&utm_content=jamanetworkopen.2020.16019.

40. V. S. Tammana, A. O. Laiyemo, "Colorectal Cancer Disparities: Issues, Controversies and Solutions," *World Journal of Gastroenterology* 20, no. 4 (January 28, 2014): 869–76, https://www.ncbi.nlm.nih.gov/pmc/articles/PMC3921540/.

41. U.S. Department of Health and Human Services Office of Minority Health, "Cancer and African Americans," accessed May 3, 2021, https://minorityhealth.hhs.gov/omh/browse.aspx?lvl=4&lvlid=16.

42. U.S. Department of Health and Human Services, "Cancer and African Americans."

43. National Kidney Foundation, "African Americans and Kidney Disease," updated January 2016, accessed May 3, 2021, https://www.kidney.org/news/newsroom/factsheets/African -Americans-and-CKD.

44. Centers for Disease Control and Prevention, "Risk for COVID-19 Infections, Hospitalization, and Death by Race/ Ethnicity," updated August 18, 2020, accessed May 3, 2021, https://www.cdc.gov/coronavirus/2019-ncov/covid-data/ investigations-discovery/hospitalization-death-by-race -ethnicity.html.

45. Rashawn Ray, Brookings Institute, FIXGOV, April 9, 2020.

46. "Health Equity Considerations and Racial and Eth- nic Minority Groups, Coronavirus Disease 2019 (COVID-19)," updated July 24, 2020, accessed May 3, 2021, https://www.cdc .gov/coronavirus/2019-ncov/community/health-equity/race -ethnicity.html.

47. Roni Caryn Rabin, "Why the Coronavirus More Often Strikes Children of Color," *New York Times*, September 1, 2020.

48. Michigan Civil Rights Commission, "The Flint Water Crisis: Systemic Racism Through the Lens of Flint; Report of the Michigan Civil Rights Commissions," February 17, 2017, 21; emphasis added.

49. *Sollicitudo Rei Socialis*; as reported by Father Fred Kam- mer, "Catholic Social Teaching (CST) and Racism," *Jesuit Social Research Institute JustSouth Quarterly* (Fall 2009): 5, http://www .loyno.edu/jsri/sites/loyno.edu.jsri/files/CSTandRacism -Fall2009jsq.pdf.

CHAPTER 6: ENVIRONMENTAL RACISM

1. United Church of Christ (UCC) Commission for Racial Justice, "Toxic Wastes and Race in the United States: A National Report on the Racial and Socio-Economic Characteristics of Communities with Hazardous Waste Sites," 1987, https://www .nrc.gov/docs/ML1310/ML13109A339.pdf.

2. UCC Commission for Racial Justice, "Toxic Wastes and Race," xiii.

3. UCC Commission for Racial Justice, "Toxic Wastes and Race," x.

4. UCC Commission for Racial Justice, "Toxic Wastes and Race," x.

5. UCC Commission for Racial Justice, "Toxic Wastes and Race," x.

6. UCC Commission for Racial Justice, "Toxic Wastes and Race," xi.

7. William K. Reilly, "Environmental Equity: EPA's Position," *EPA Journal* 18, no. 9 (March/April 1992); as reported in Robert D. Bullard et al., "Toxic Wastes and Race at Twenty, 1987–2007: A Report Prepared for the United Church of Christ Justice and Witness Ministries" (2007), 4, https://www.researchgate.net/profile/Robin-Saha/publication/285677217_Toxic_wastes_and _race_at_twenty_1987-2007_A_report_prepared_for_the_United _Church_of_christ_justice_and_witness_ministries/links/ 5f7e1cb3a6fdccfd7b4f620a/Toxic-wastes-and-race-at-twenty -1987-2007-A-report-prepared-for-the-United-Church-of-christ -justice-and-witness-ministries.pdf.

8. R. D. Bullard and B. H. Wright, "The Politics of Pollution: Implications for the Black Community," *Phylon* 47 (March 1986): 71–78; as reported in Bullard et al., "Toxic Wastes and Race at Twenty," 4.

9. Julian Agyeman, Robert D. Bullard, and Bob Evans, "Just Sustainabilities: Development in An Unequal World," MIT Press (2003); as reported in Bullard et al., "Toxic Wastes and Race at Twenty," 4.

10. Bullard et al., "Toxic Wastes and Race at Twenty," 4.

11. U.S. Environmental Protection Agency, "Release of Environmental Equity Report," Press Release (1992).

12. U.S. Environmental Protection Agency, "Release of Environmental Equity Report," Press Release (2007), xii.

13. Michigan Civil Rights Commission, "The Flint Water Crisis: Systemic Racism Through the Lens of Flint; Report of the Michigan Civil Rights Commissions," February 17, 2017.

14. David Eggert, Ed White, and Corey Williams, "Ex-Governor, Eight Others Charged in Flint Water Probe," *Philadelphia Inquirer*, January 15, 2021.

15. Bryan N. Massingale, *Racial Justice and the Catholic Church* (Maryknoll, NY: Orbis Books, 2010), 41.

CHAPTER 7: VOTER SUPPRESSION

1. Equal Justice Institute (EJI), *Lynching in America: Confronting the Legacy of Racial Terror*, 3rd ed. (Montgomery, AL: Equal Justice Institute, 2017), 10–11; based in part on Henry Lewis Gates's *Stoney the Road: Reconstruction, White Supremacy and the Rise of Jim Crow* (New York: Penguin Press, 2019).

2. "Race and Voting in the Segregated South," Constitutional Rights Foundation, accessed May 4, 2021, https://www.crf-usa.org/black-history-month/race-and-voting-in-the-segregated-south.

3. Carol Anderson, *One Person, No Vote: How Voter Suppression Is Destroying Our Democracy* (New York: Bloomsbury Publishing, 2018), 3.

4. Michael Waldman, *The Fight to Vote* (New York: Simon and Schuster, 2016), 85, 89; as reported in Anderson, *One Person, No Vote*, 3.

5. Waldman, *The Fight to Vote*; as reported in Anderson, *One Person, No Vote*, 3.

6. Waldman, *The Fight to Vote*; as reported in Anderson, *One Person, No Vote*, 4.

7. Waldman, *The Fight to Vote*; as reported in Anderson, *One Person, No Vote*, 4.

8. Waldman, *The Fight to Vote*; as reported in Anderson, *One Person, No Vote*, 4.

9. Waldman, *The Fight to Vote*; as reported in Anderson, *One Person, No Vote*, 7.

10. Waldman, *The Fight to Vote*; as reported in Anderson, *One Person, No Vote*, 16.

11. Waldman, *The Fight to Vote*; as reported in Anderson, *One Person, No Vote*, 16.

12. Waldman, *The Fight to Vote*; as reported in Anderson, *One Person, No Vote*, 16.

13. Waldman, *The Fight to Vote*; as reported in Anderson, *One Person, No Vote*, 16.

14. Charles S. Bullock III, Ronald Keith Gaddie, and Justin J. Wert, *The Rise and Fall of the Voting Rights Act* (Norman: University of Oklahoma Press, 2016), 18; as reported in Anderson, *One Person, No Vote*, 21.

15. Alexander Keysarr, *The Right to Vote: The Contested History of Democracy in the United States* (New York: Basic Books, 2000), 212; as reported in Anderson, *One Person, No Vote*, 27.

16. Vann R. Newkirk II, "How Shelby County v. Holder Broke America," *The Atlantic*, July 10, 2018.

17. Justin Levitt, "The Truth about Voter Fraud," Brennan Center for Justice, November 9, 2007, https://www.brennancenter.org/our-work/research-reports/truth-about-voter-fraud.

18. Justin Levitt, "A Comprehensive Investigation of Voter Impersonation Finds 31 Credible Incidents Out of One Billion Ballots Cast," *Washington Post*, August 6, 2014.

19. Douglas Keith, Myrna Perez, and Christopher Famighetti, "Noncitizen Voting: The Missing Millions," Brennan Center for Justice, May 5, 2017, https://www.brennancenter.org/our-work/research-reports/noncitizen-voting-missing-millions.

20. Brennan Center for Justice, "New Voting Restrictions in America," October 1, 2019, updated November 19, 2019, https://www.brennancenter.org/our-work/research-reports/new-voting-restrictions-america.

21. Brennan Center for Justice, "New Voting Restrictions in America."

22. Keysarr, *The Right to Vote*, 284; as reported in Anderson, *One Person, No Vote*, 52.

23. Benjamin Roth, *The Great Depression: A Diary*, ed. James Ledbetter and Daniel B. Roth (New York: Public Affairs, 2009), 23; as reported in Anderson, *One Person, No Vote*, 52.

24. Anderson, *One Person, No Vote*, foreword.

25. Christopher Uggen, Sarah Shannon, and Jeff Manza, "State-Level Estimates of Felon Disenfranchisement in the United

States, 2010," The Sentencing Project, July 12, 2012, https://www.sentencingproject.org/publications/state-level-estimates-of-felon-disenfranchisement-in-the-united-states-2010/.

26. Ari Berman, "How the 2000 Election in Florida Led to a New Wave of Voter Disenfranchisement," *The Nation*, July 28, 2015.

27. Jim Rutenberg, Nick Corasaniti, and Alan Feuer, "Trump's Failed Crusade Debunks GOP's Case for Voting Restrictions—Over and Over, Courts Find No Fraud, but Efforts to Limit Rights Persist," *New York Times*, December 27, 2020.

28. Brennan Center for Justice, "Refuting the Myth of Voter Fraud Yet Again," January 6, 2021, https://www.brennancenter.org/our-work/research-reports/refuting-myth-voter-fraud-yet-again.

29. Brennan Center for Justice, "Voting Laws Roundup: March 2021," April 1, 2021, https://www.brennancenter.org/our-work/research-reports/voting-laws-roundup-march-2021.

30. Pope Francis's address to the U.S. Congress, September 24, 2015; see Committee on Cultural Diversity in the Church of the USCCB, "Open Wide Our Hearts: The Enduring Call to Love; A Pastoral Letter Against Racism," November 2018, 28.

CHAPTER 8: WEALTH AND INCOME DISPARITIES

1. Dedrick Asante-Muhammad, Chuck Collins, Josh Hoxie, and Sabrina Terry, "Dreams Deferred: How Enriching the 1% Widens the Racial Wealth Divide," Institute for Policy Studies, January 14, 2019, 9, https://inequality.org/great-divide/dreams-deferred-racial-wealth-divide/.

2. Douglas A. Blackmon, *Slavery by Another Name: The Re-Enslavement of Black Americans from the Civil War to World War II* (New York: Anchor Books, 2008), 7.

3. Message from the Board of Directors, "80 Years of New Beginnings," UNICOR Federal Prison Industries, Inc., accessed May 5, 2021, https://www.unicor.gov/Publications/Corporate/CATC6500_FINAL_20160114.pdf.

4. Wendy Sawyer, "How Much Do Incarcerated People Earn in Each State?," Prison Policy Initiative, April 10, 2017, https://www.prisonpolicy.org/blog/2017/04/10/wages/; as reported in Ben Crump, *Open Season: Legalized Genocide of Colored People* (New York: HarperCollins Books, 2019), 190.

5. Blackmon, *Slavery by Another Name*, 66.

6. Grif Stockley, "Elaine Massacre of 1919," Butler Center for Arkansas Studies, February 6, 2019.

7. Personal experience of Vince Gallagher during safety inspections conducted for the Occupational Safety and Health Administration and investigation of accidents he conducted in more than one thousand factories in the United States over forty years.

8. Sue Pollack and JoAnn Grozuczak, *Reagan, Toxics, and Minorities: A Policy Report* (Washington, DC: Urban Environment Conference, 1984).

9. Ivette Perfecto, "Pesticide Exposure and Farm Workers and the International Connection," in *Race and the Incidence of Environmental Hazards*, ed. Bunyan Bryant and Paul Mohai (Boulder, CO: West View Press, 1992).

10. Marion Mosses, "Pesticide-Related Health Problems in Farm Workers," *American Association of Occupational Health Nurses Journal* 37 (1989): 115–30.

11. Beverly H. Wright, "The Effects of Occupational Injury, Illness, and Disease and the Health Status of Black Americans: A Review," in Bryant and Mohai, eds., *Race and the Incidence of Environmental Hazards*.

12. Larry Williams, "Long-Term Mortality of Steel Workers; I: Methodology," *Journal of Occupational Medicine* 2 (1969): 301.

13. Nora Lapin and Karen Hoffman, *Occupational Disease among Workers: An Annotated Bibliography* (Hyattsville, MD: National Institute of Occupational Safety and Health, 1981).

14. Benjamin A. Goldman, *The Truth about Where You Live: An Atlas for Action on Toxins and Mortality* (New York: Time Books/Random House, 1991).

15. Nikole Hannah-Jones, "What Is Owed," *New York Times Magazine* (June 30, 2020).

16. Lizzie Presser, "The Dispossessed: Why So Many Black Families Are Losing Their Property," *The New Yorker* (July 15, 2019): 29.

17. Todd Lewan, Delores Barclay, and Allen G. Breed, "Landownership Made Blacks Targets of Violence and Murder," Associated Press, December 3, 2001; available at the Authentic Voice, accessed May 5, 2021, https://theauthenticvoice.org/mainstories/tornfromtheland/torn_part2/.

18. Heirs Property Retention Coalition, accessed May 5, 2021, http://hprc.southerncoalition.org/?q=node/5.

19. Leah Douglas, "African Americans Have Lost Untold Acres of Land Over the Last Century," *The Nation* (July 17–24, 2017).

20. Douglas, "African Americans Have Lost Untold Acres."

21. Presser, "The Dispossessed," 29.

22. Richard Rothstein, *The Color of Law: A Forgotten History of How Our Government Segregated America* (New York: Liveright Publishing, 2017), 156.

23. Hannah-Jones, "What Is Owed."

24. Rothstein, *The Color of Law*, 156.

25. Rothstein, *The Color of Law*, 157.

26. Rothstein, *The Color of Law*, 159.

27. Ira Katznelson, *When Affirmative Action Was White* (New York: W. W. Norton and Company, 2005), 115.

28. Katznelson, *When Affirmative Action Was White*, 140.

29. Rothstein, *The Color of Law*, 167.

30. Redlining is a discriminatory practice by which banks, insurance companies, and other institutions or organizations refuse or limit loans, mortgages, insurance, and so on within specific geographic areas, especially in inner-city neighborhoods.

31. "The Plunder of Black Wealth in Chicago: New Findings on the Lasting Toll of Predatory Housing Contracts," the Samuel DeBois Cook Center on Social Equity, Duke University; as reported in the *Chicago Reporter* (June 6, 2019).

32. Rothstein, *The Color of Law*, 97.

33. Rothstein, *The Color of Law*, 170.

34. Rothstein, *The Color of Law*, 171.

35. Rothstein, *The Color of Law*, 171.

36. Rothstein, *The Color of Law*, 171.

37. Rothstein, *The Color of Law*, 172.

38. The Inquirer Editorial Board, "Robbing Philadelphia of Its Wealth," *Philadelphia Inquirer*, January 2, 2020.

39. Andre Perry, Jonathan Rothwell, and David Harshbarger, "The Devaluation of Assets in Black Neighborhoods: The Case of Residential Property," Metropolitan Policy Program at Brookings, November 27, 2018, https://www.brookings.edu/research/devaluation-of-assets-in-black-neighborhoods/.

40. Amy Traub, Catherine Ruetschlin, Laura Sullivan, Tatjina Meschede, et al., "The Racial Wealth Gap: Why Policy Matters," June 21, 2016, 1, https://www.demos.org/publication/racial-wealth-gap-why-policy-matters.

41. Janelle Jones, "The Racial Wealth Gap: How African Americans Have Been Shortchanged Out of the Materials to Build Wealth," Economic Policy Institute, February 13, 2017, https://www.epi.org/blog/the-racial-wealth-gap-how-african-americans-have-been-shortchanged-out-of-the-materials-to-build-wealth/.

42. Ta-Nehisi Coates, "The Case for Reparations," *The Atlantic*, June 2014.

43. Andrew Woo and Chris Salviati, "Imbalance in Housing Aid: Mortgage Interest Deduction vs. Section 8," *Rentonomics*, October 11, 2017.

44. Jackie Stein, "Fighting for a U.S. Federal Budget that Prioritizes Peace, Economic Security, and Shared Prosperity—The Home Mortgage Interest Deduction: Who Benefits?" National Priorities Project, July 8, 2013, https://www.nationalpriorities.org/blog/2013/07/08/home-mortgage-interest-deduction-who-benefits/.

45. Richard V. Reeves, *Dream Hoarders* (Washington, DC: Brookings Institution Press, 2017), 105.

46. Ezra Levin, "Upside Down: Homeownership Tax Programs," Corporation for Enterprise Development, September 2014, accessed May 6, 2021, https://studylib.net/doc/8200083/upside-down--homeownership-tax-programs; as reported in Reeves, *Dream Hoarders*, 151.

47. Levin, "Upside Down: Homeownership Tax Programs"; as reported in Reeves, *Dream Hoarders*, 151.

48. "The Distribution of Major Tax Exemptions in the Individual Tax System" (see Congressional Budget Office, 2013), https://www.cbo.gov/publication/43768; as reported by Christian E. Weller and Teresa Ghilarducci, "The Inefficiencies of Existing Retirement Savings Incentives," Center for American Progress (October 29, 2015), https://www.americanprogress .org/issues/economy/reports/2015/10/30/124315/the -inefficiencies-of-existing-retirement-savings-incentives/.

49. Weller and Ghilarducci, "Inefficiencies of Existing Retirement Savings Incentives," 2.

50. Beadsie Woo, Ida Rademacher, and Jillien Meier, "Upside Down: The $400 Billion Federal Asset Building Budget," CFED and The Annie E. Casey Foundation (2010); as reported in Laura Sullivan, Tatjana Meschede, Lars Dietrich, and Thomas Shapiro, "The Racial Wealth Gap: Why Policy Matters," Institute for Asset and Social Policy, Brandeis University—Demos, June 21, 2016, https://www.demos.org/sites/default/files/publications/ RacialWealthGap_2.pdf.

51. Janelle Jones, John Schmitt, and Valerie Wilson, "50 Years after the Kerner Commission: African Americans Are Better Off in Many Ways but Are Still Disadvantaged by Racial Inequality," Economic Policy Institute, February 26, 2018, https://www.epi .org/publication/50-years-after-the-kerner-commission/.

52. Urban Institute, "Nine Charts about Wealth Inequality in America (Updated)," Urban Institute, updated October 5, 2017, accessed May 6, 2021, https://apps.urban.org/features/ wealth-inequality-charts/; calculations are taken from "Survey of Financial Characteristics of Consumers 1962 (December 31)," "Survey of Changes in Family Finances 1963," and "Survey of Consumer Finances 1983–2016."

53. Urban Institute, "Nine Charts."

54. Louis W. Diuguid, *Discovering the Real America: Toward a More Perfect Union* (Boca Raton, FL: Brown Walker Press, 2007), 84.

55. Sendhil Mullainathan, "The Measuring Strips of Racial Bias," *New York Times,* January 4, 2015.

56. Eddie S. Glaude Jr., *Democracy in Black: How Race Still Enslaves the American Soul* (New York: Crown Publishers, 2016), 19, 20.

57. Glaude, *Democracy in Black,* 20.

58. "Brothers and Sisters to Us," U.S. Catholic Bishops, 1979.

CHAPTER 9: RESTORATIVE JUSTICE

1. Roy L. Brooks, *Integration or Separation? A Strategy for Racial Equality* (Cambridge, MA: Harvard University Press, 1996), ix; as reported in Roy L. Brooks, *Atonement and Forgiveness: A New Model for Black Reparation* (Berkeley: University of California Press, 2004), 36.

2. Nikole Hannah-Jones, "What Is Owed," *New York Times Magazine* (June 26, 2020).

3. Bianca DiJulio et al., "Survey of Americans on Race," Kaiser Family Foundation/CNN, November 24, 2015, https://www.kff.org/other/report/survey-of-americans-on-race/.

4. Eddie S. Glaude Jr., *Democracy in Black: How Race Still Enslaves the American Soul* (New York: Crown Publishers, 2016), 87.

5. The Inquirer Editorial Board, "Frederick Douglass' 'What to the Slave Is the Fourth of July?'" (Douglass' speech delivered July 5, 1852), *Philadelphia Inquirer*, July 4, 2020.

6. Hannah-Jones, "What Is Owed."

7. Chuck Collins, Dedrick Asante-Muhammed, Josh Hoxie, and Sabrina Terry, "Dreams Deferred: How Enriching the One Percent Widens the Racial Wealth Divide," Institute for Policy Studies, January 15, 2019, https://ips-dc.org/racial-wealth-divide-2019/.

8. Dylan Matthews, "Study: Cory Booker's Baby Bonds Nearly Close the Racial Wealth Gap for Young Adults," Vox, updated February 1, 2019, accessed May 7, 2021, https://www.vox.com/future-perfect/2019/1/21/18185536/cory-booker-news-today-2020-presidential-election-baby-bonds.

9. Pontifical Council for Justice and Peace, "The Church and Racism: Toward a More Fraternal Society," no. 25; as reported in Dawn Nothwehr, *That They May Be One: Catholic Social Teaching on Racism, Tribalism and Xenophobia* (Maryknoll, NY: Orbis Books, 2008), 64.

CHAPTER 10: THE POWER OF STORY

1. *Solicitudo Rei Socialis*; as reported in Bryan N. Massingale, *Racial Justice and the Catholic Church* (Maryknoll, NY: Orbis Books, 2010), 116.

2. "Open Wide Our Hearts: The Enduring Call of Love, A Pastoral Letter against Racism," U.S. Conference of Catholic Bishops (USCCB), General Meeting, November 2018, developed by the Committee on Cultural Diversity.

CHAPTER 11: REPAIRING THE WOUNDED HEART

1. "Open Wide Our Hearts: The Enduring Call of Love, A Pastoral Letter against Racism," U.S. Conference of Catholic Bishops (USCCB), General Meeting, November 2018, developed by the Committee on Cultural Diversity.

INDEX

Index